"This apple, dear Sisters, is a token of everything that arouses lust and sensual delights." Ancren Riwle, *a handbook for nuns, circa 1200*

This contemporary cookbook is a unique addition to either the cookbook shelf or the coffee table. The recipes are divided into two main categories: ancient and modern. The modern recipes were concocted by the Fraziers in their San Francisco kitchen. The ancient recipes and the adages which accompany them were lovingly researched from old books, documents and records. The book contains a complete history of love foods, from a variety of cultures, including Chinese, Arabic, Latin American, Greek and Roman.

APHRODISIAC COOKERY

Ancient & Modern

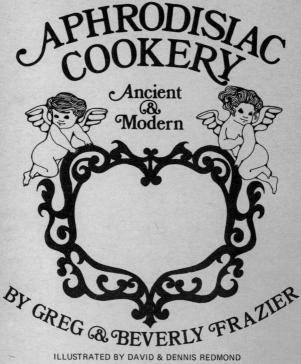

BY GREG & BEVERLY FRAZIER

ILLUSTRATED BY DAVID & DENNIS REDMOND

WARNER

PAPERBACK LIBRARY
NEW YORK

Dedicated
to
The One I Love

WARNER PAPERBACK LIBRARY EDITION
First Printing: January, 1973

Copyright © 1970 by Greg and Beverly Frazier
All rights reserved

Library of Congress Catalog Card Number: 71-128534

This Warner Paperback Library Edition is published by arrangement
with Troubador Press, Inc.

Cover photograph by Paul Weller

Warner Paperback Library is a division of Warner Books, Inc.,
315 Park Avenue South, New York, N.Y. 10010.

CONTENTS

FOREWORD

If there is a primary lesson to be learned from the study of aphrodisiacs and erotic cookery, it is this: *It is not what the food brings to you, it is what you bring to the food.* The effectiveness of the aphrodisiac is in direct proportion to your cultural and personal belief in it. If you firmly believe, as did the ancient Romans, that shallots from Megara will enhance your sexual prowess, then in all probability they will. The recipes in this book worked for us because we *believed* they would work, and because they were taken in a spirit of mutual love.

The recipes are of two kinds: ancient and modern. The ancient recipes were compiled from folklore and literature. Since the ancients often sought only to stimulate the passions and not necessarily the palate, some of these archaic concoctions may seem unappetizing, if not noxious. They are included only as curios of man's unceasing search for love foods. We do not recommend that you try these ancient philtres. We do recommend, however, that before testing the recipes you read the introductory material preceding each chapter. It is in these introductory passages that the amazing story of aphrodisiacs unfolds. Bon amour!

Greg and Beverly Frazier
San Francisco

INTRODUCTION

Aphrodisiacs are substances capable of stimulating sexual desire. They are named after Aphrodite, the Greek goddess of love. They include, in addition to those substances taken internally, visual, aural, tactile and olfactory stimulants; in short, *anything* that excites sexuality. Aphrodisiacs have occupied the searches and researches of man from ancient to modern times, and almost no culture, primitive or civilized, is without its pharmacopoeia of love foods.

Probably the earliest recorded mention of aphrodisiacs comes from undated Egyptian medical papyri believed to be from the Middle Kingdom which flourished between 2200–1700 B.C. Aphrodisiacs are mentioned in the *Bible* and many of the world's sacred books, so that those who make a moral issue out of their use do not base their objections on literary reality. Ancient literature is filled with glowing accounts of aphrodisiac foods, and, by the time of the Golden Age of Greece, their use was fairly commonplace. The Romans, who inherited their culture from the Greeks, were also intimately familiar with the art of culinary seduction. Aphrodisiac lore passed from the Romans to the early Christian era, the Middle Ages, the Renaissance, and into modern times. Today we are bombarded by advertisements alleging that certain products enhance sexuality, advertisements that echo in contemporary terms the claims of the most ancient of aphrodisiacs. This is not to say that aphrodisiacs are strictly a Western phenomenon. Simultaneous with the proliferation of love foods in the Western world was a corresponding awareness of their powers in the mystic East; in fact, some connoisseurs insist that Oriental aphrodisiacs are among the most potent.

Modern science lends little credibility to the belief in the stimulating properties of foods, recognizing only two "true" aphrodisiacs; cantharides (Spanish fly), and yohimbine, a yellowish powder derived from the bark of the yohimbe tree. Science does, however, recognize the psychological lure of aphrodisiacs. Many psychologists maintain that aphrodisiacs will work if one *believes* they will work. The psychological connection between food and sex is well known in scientific circles.

When one speaks of the "hunger" for food and the "hunger" for sex, he is hinting profoundly at the inseparable physical and psychological relationship between these two of man's most basic needs. Somewhere over the long evolutionary process the need to find food and sexual expression have merged and become confused in man's psyche. This psychological short-circuiting has resulted in the concept of the "Doctrine of Signatures" (the ancient belief in the therapeutic efficacy of resemblances), and sympathetic magic, today described as the "you-are-what-you-eat" syndrome. Primitive man copulated in the fields in the belief that the crops would share his fertility. He observed the sexual behavior of animals and deduced that if one ate the flesh of the more virile species the virility would be passed on to the consumer. It didn't take a genius to conclude that eating the sexual parts of the animal would be even more effective. Foods that resembled, tasted, or smelled like the male and female genitalia were also used as aphrodisiacs. One person may include the carrot among the most erotic of foods; another is stimulated by the appearance and mucous texture of raw oysters; and a third is sent into ecstasy by a cream puff.

Set (attitude), setting (atmosphere), and the power of suggestion are primary considerations when plying a loved one with aphrodisiacs. When Madame Du Barry fed her amber-spiked bon-bons to the aging Louis XV, she was undoubtedly sure to mention, quite casually, that the recipe for those delicious tidbits was handed down by an Arabian sheikh who not only satisfied a harem of 150 concubines, but also managed to deflower twice eighty virgins in a fortnight. Her elegant table was most likely laden with rich and succulent foods, served by candlelight to the romantic strains of the court fiddlers. And as the voluptuous Madame purred her deceit into the old king's ear, his "spirits" were certain to rise.

Surely, eating, like sex, is most enjoyable when all of the senses are called into play, making a feast for the total organism. The combination of various sensuous reactions — the visual satisfaction at the sight of appetizing foods, their pleasing aroma and varying consistencies — tend to create a state of euphoria conducive to sexual expression. Even the most naive schoolboy, out on his first date, is well aware of the seductive atmosphere of candlelight and wine.

The French, gourmets and lovers all, have made a veritable art of culinary seduction. In the 19th century many Parisian restaurants featured private dining rooms, called *cabinets particuliers,* which catered to the more amorously inclined customers. These dining-cum-boudoir suites were luxuriously furnished and specialized in creating an atmosphere rich in sensual delights. The bed was a mere few feet from the table, making the transition from sitting to lying an easy one. These sumptuous establishments may have been unique to the French, but they were not unique to France.

In the Gay Nineties, during the champagne days of San Francisco, many similar French restaurants with "upstairs suites" were the pride and scandal of the city. The bill of fare included oysters Kirkpatrick, broiled terrapin, and fourteen-course dinners served with seven varieties of wine. The customer could choose from the live frogs displayed in the windows for his dish of frog's legs à la poulette. After seducing their palates with fine foods, a gentleman and his lady would climax the evening in one of the canopied beds discretely supplied by the management. The proprietors of these love nests were well instructed on the erotic results of a satisfying meal by the Marquis de Sade: "A plenteous meal may produce voluptuous sensations."

Nowhere is the psychological relationship between food and sex more evident than in language. Many terms for food have sexual connotations. These terms, called erotolabia, appear in English and other foreign languages and their existence is no mere accident, but proof of man's universal preoccupation with the erotic character of foods. Words like "cherry", "nuts", "wiener", "dish", "tart", to name but a few, refer to some aspect of human sexuality. Others, like "sweetheart" and "dumpling" are used as terms of affection. Food, sex, and language are all intricately entwined in a psychological maze providing literal food for thought.

The marriage of food and sex is not only psychological, but physical as well. Before eating, animals salivate to prepare the mouth and esophagus to receive food in much the same way that the sexual organs secrete mucous before coitus. The German nutritionist, Balzli, points out that, "the sensual internal surface areas of the sex organs, correspond to the taste-buds of the mouth." Certain nerve structures which are extremely sensitive to stimulation, called "Krause's end-bulbs," are found principally in the penis, clitoris — and lips. Man's urge to engage in oral-genital contact is as natural and healthy as his desire to partake of tasty and satisfying foods. As the Song of Solomon so poetically puts it: "I sat down under his shadow, whom I desired: and his fruit was sweet to my palate."

The list of aphrodisiac foods ranges from the exotic to the commonplace. Even such unromantic items as the potato and the bean were once considered powerful love stimulants. The idea that a potato in the dining room can lead to a frolic in the bedroom is not as ridiculous as it sounds. Take the strange case of the barbasco.

The barbasco is a wild yam native to Mexico, Central and South America, Africa and India. From the roots of the barbasco is extracted the basis for many modern drugs, including diosgenin, a steroid chemical used in the manufacture of birth control pills. In the laboratory, diosgenin is transformed into a *synthetic sex hormone*. Prior to the discovery of this amazing chemical, one European firm had to process a ton of bull's testicles to produce 1/100 of an ounce of a certain type of sex hormone. Sex hormones *do* have an aphrodisiac effect; they are used to treat frigidity and impotence in humans. Is it inconceivable, in this cybernetic era of space flight and miracle drugs, that some brilliant scientist will extract a true aphrodisiac from a common food like the bean or potato?

All sensation is ultimately located in the brain. We already have drugs that can stimulate, tranquilize, and depress. If there is a button in the brain's control panel marked SEX, then there is a substance to push it, even if it is as yet undiscovered. Time, which brings knowledge, is all that separates the modern chemist from the ancient alchemist.

MEASUREMENTS

Dash: 1/8 teaspoon
Pinch: As much as can be taken between finger tips

3 teaspoons	1 tablespoon
2 tablespoons	1/8 cup
4 tablespoons	¼ cup
8 tablespoons	½ cup
16 tablespoons	1 cup
4 ounces	½ cup
8 ounces	1 cup
2 cups	1 pint
2 pints	1 quart
1 quart	4 cups
2 cups sugar	1 pound
1 pound butter	2 cups

OVEN TEMPERATURES

250° to 325°	Slow oven
325° to 375°	Moderate oven
375° to 425°	Moderately hot oven
425° to 475°	Hot oven
475° to 500°	Very hot oven

ABBREVIATIONS

t	teaspoon
T	tablespoon
lb.	pound
oz.	ounce
pt.	pint
qt.	quart

Fruits and nuts, those gifts of nature which contain the very seeds of life, have been for countless ages associated with fertility and abundance. The ancients believed that the fertility of the tree would be passed on magically to whomever ate the tree's first fruit. This magic by association, basic to the belief in the aphrodisiac qualities of food, is dramatically illustrated in the Biblical account of the Fall of Man. "And the woman saw that the tree was good to eat, and fair to the eyes, and delightful to behold: and she took of the fruit thereof, and did eat, and gave to her husband, who did eat." Thus man fell from the grace of God, acquired the knowledge of Good and Evil, became ashamed, and covered his nakedness with a fig leaf.

The story of Adam and Eve is not unique to the *Bible,* however. *The Bundehesh,* a sacred book of the Persians, contains an almost identical account of the Fall. Ahuramazda, after creating Mashya and Mashyana, the first man and woman, bade them to be pure in thoughts, speech and actions. But an evil demon came to them in the form of a serpent, sent by Ahriman, the prince of devils, who gave them fruit of a magical tree which imparted immortality. After eating the forbidden fruit they fell into moral decay, became ashamed, and covered their nakedness with the skins of animals.

Man's insatiable curiosity, which tempted Eve to taste the forbidden fruit, later led the philosophers into heated dispute over *which* fruit was responsible for man's exile from Paradise. Nowhere does the *Bible* mention an apple as the forbidden fruit. It simply alludes to "the fruit of the Tree of Knowledge." St. Jerome, in the 4th century A.D., was the first to state unequivocally that the apple was the culprit. Medieval artists re-enforced this belief by painting Eve with an apple in her hand. Milton, in *Paradise Lost,* says that the first act of Adam and Eve after tasting the apple was to make love in a bed of flowers. So the first man and woman lost one paradise only to find another. Through their lustful behavior the apple became the symbol of earthly desires and an aphrodisiac of the highest quality.

Because of their power to bestow fertility and virility, fruits and nuts have always played a prominent role in wedding ceremonies the world over. Nuts were given to newlyweds in ancient Rome; in modern Europe and America no marriage is complete without the traditional gift of almonds from the bride. Oranges and grapes, because of their prolific number of seeds, were given to the bride and groom in the belief that they would bless the marriage with many children. Pomegranates were valued because they were thought to have sprung from the blood of Dionysus, the Greek god of wine. Bananas and figs are considered love stimulants among many primitive peoples due to their genital appearance.

If the apple of your eye is reluctant to share his fruits, try an offering of nuts.

The apple, which I received from the hand
Of the most charming, gazelle-like maiden,
Which she had plucked herself from a branch
That was as supple as her own body.
And sweet it was to place my hand upon it
As though it was the breast of the one who gave it.
Pure was the fragrance of the apple,
Like the breath of the giver.
One could see the color of her cheek on it,
And I thought I was tasting her lips
When I began to eat the apple.

—9th century Arabic poem

LINGAM SAUSAGE IN APPLE YONI

4 cooking apples, cored
1 cup brown sugar
½ cup water
½ t cinnamon
8 pork sausages
4 sprigs fresh mint

Peel apples halfway. In large kettle combine sugar, water and cinnamon. Stir until sugar is dissolved; add apples and cook in syrup for 5 minutes. Remove apples and place in baking dish. Place 2 sausages in center of each apple and pour syrup over top. Bake in 350° oven for 40 minutes or until sausage is thoroughly cooked. Garnish with mint. Serves 4.

. . . but that false Fruit
Farr other operation first displaid,
Carnal desire enflaming, hee on Eve
Began to cast lascivious Eyes, she him
As wantonly repaid; in Lust they burne:
Till Adam *thus 'gan* Eve *to dalliance move . . .*

Her hand he seis'd, and to a shadie bank,
Thick overhead with verdant roof imbowr'd
He led her nothing loath;
Flours were the Couch,
Pansies, and Violets, and Asphodel,
And Hyacinth, Earths freshest softest lap.
There they thir fill of Love and Loves disport
Took largely, of thir mutual guilt the Seale,
The solace of thir sin, till dewie sleep
Oppress'd them, wearied with thir amorous play.

— Milton,
describing the aphrodisiac effects of
the Forbidden Fruit.
Paradise Lost, *1667*

FORBIDDEN FRUIT

8 large cooking apples
   Sugar to taste
1 t cinnamon
1 T butter
4 eggs, beaten

Peel and slice apples and stew until very tender. Drain and mash thoroughly. Stir in sugar, cinnamon and butter. Set aside. When apple mixture has cooled, stir in eggs. Heat additional butter in skillet and drop mixture by spoonfuls in hot butter. Brown lightly on both sides. Sprinkle with sugar. Serves 6.

An apple, an egg and a nut
You may eat after a slut.

— John Ray,
English Proverbs, *1670*

APPLE CAKE IN THE RAW

4 cups diced raw apples, peeled
½ cup shortening
2 cups sugar
2 eggs, beaten
1 cup chopped nuts
½ cup raisins
2 cups unsifted flour
2 t soda
1 t salt
1 t cinnamon
1 t nutmeg
1 t vanilla

Cream shortening and sugar. Add beaten eggs and vanilla. Mix well. Stir in remaining ingredients. Place mixture into well greased 8 x 12 inch baking dish. Bake in 325° oven for 1 hour. Sprinkle hot cake with sugar and serve.

GARDEN OF EDEN SALAD

3 large red apples, unpeeled and diced
3/4 cup diced celery
½ cup chopped pecans
½ cup mayonnaise
2 t lemon juice
3/4 t ginger

In large bowl combine mayonnaise, lemon juice and ginger. Fold in apples, celery and pecans. Serve on crisp lettuce leaves and garnish with pecan halves. Serves 6.

If, my pet, you gave me these two apples as tokens of your breasts, I bless you for your great kindness. But if your gift does not go beyond the apples, you wrong me by refusing to quench the fierce fire you lit.

— Paulus Silentiarius,
6th century Greek poet

HEAVEN AND EARTH

4 small potatoes, peeled and sliced
2 small apples, peeled and sliced
1 t salt
2 T butter
3 slices bacon, minced
½ onion, minced

In large kettle boil potatoes and apples in salted water. Drain and mash with butter. In small skillet saute bacon and onion until lightly browned. Top potatoes with sauteed bacon and onion. Serve with sausages or roast pork. Serves 4.

thes eppel, leove sustren, bitocneth alle the thing lust falleth to delit of sunne.

This apple, dear Sisters, is a token of everything that arouses lust and sensual delights.

— Ancren Riwle,
a handbook for nuns,
circa 1200

The peach, with its deep and opulent cleft, was a symbol of the female genitalia to the ancient Chinese, and its sweet juice symbolized the effluvia of the Yin. Chinese brides were also called "peaches."

YIN AND YANG PEACHES

2 oz. ground toasted almonds
6 T powdered sugar
1 T chopped glazed orange peel
12 peach halves
½ cup sherry
   Sweetened whipped cream

Combine almonds, 3 T sugar and orange peel. Fill peach halves
with almond mixture and place in baking dish. Sprinkle
peaches with remaining sugar and pour sherry over top. Bake
in 350° oven for 10 minutes. Serve warm and top with
whipped cream. Serves 6.

*Venus owns this [peach] tree ... the fruit provokes lust ... If
the kernels be bruised and boiled in vinegar until they become
thick, and applied to the head, it marvelously makes the hair
to grow again upon the bald places or where it is too thin.*
                                                  – Nicholas Culpeper,
                               – Culpeper's Complete Herbal, 1652

PEACH AMBROSIA PIE

1 baked pie shell, cooled
1 package orange gelatin
1¼ cups hot water
1 pt. peach ice cream
1 cup fresh diced peaches
¼ cup sugar
½ pt. heavy cream, sweetened and whipped
   Flake coconut

Dissolve gelatin in hot water and slowly add ice cream, stirring
until dissolved. Chill mixture until slightly thickened. Mix
peaches with sugar and fold into gelatin. Pour into pie shell.
Top with whipped cream and sprinkle with coconut. Chill.
Serves 6.

The ancients associated figs with phallic worship, and figs were consumed with lusty abandon at the Greek love orgy of Dionysia. Among the Hindus, the fig is a symbol of the lingam and yoni (male and female genitalia). The French expression faire la figue *refers to an obscene gesture made with the thumb and two fingers.*

FARE à la FIG

½ cup chopped dried figs
1 8 oz. can crushed pineapple, undrained
½ cup chopped walnuts
½ cup miniature marshmallows
1½ cups cold cooked rice
1 cup sour cream

Combine first five ingredients. Fold in sour cream and chill. Serves 6.

*Now live splendidly together
Free from adversity.
Pick [your] figs
May his be large and hard,
May hers be sweet!*

– *Aristophanes,*
The Peace, *421 B.C.*

FRIPPERY FIG TOPPING

1½ cups chopped dried figs
½ cup light brown sugar
1 cup water
½ cup chopped walnuts
   Coffee ice cream

Simmer figs, sugar and water until figs are soft and sauce is slightly thickened. Cool. Stir in nuts. Serve over coffee ice cream.

Eat the banana;
I look at him;
I give him the banana.
As the banana is with me now,
So will the man be with me.

— *Lossu (New Ireland)*
love recitation

MERRY WIDOW SALAD

2 bananas
2 sliced pineapple rings
2 maraschino cherries
  Crisped lettuce
  Mayonnaise

If necessary, shave banana to slip into hole of pineapple. Place pineapple ring on bed of lettuce and stand banana in ring. Top with cherry and serve with mayonnaise thinned with pineapple juice. Serves 2.

> *Banish every evil, be lovable, in order to be loved.*
>
> — *Ovid,*
> **Ars Amatoria**

Where the banana grows man is sensual and cruel.

— *Ralph Waldo Emerson,*
Society and Solitude, *1870*

BANANA-NUT SALAD

4 small bananas
½ cup chopped celery
½ cup chopped peanuts
 Lemon juice
¼ t salt
¼ t paprika
½ cup Ginger Cheese Dressing

Slice bananas and sprinkle with lemon juice. Add celery, nuts, salt and paprika. Toss with dressing. Chill. Serves 4.

GINGER CHEESE DRESSING

¼ cup oil
¼ cup lemon juice
2 T honey
2 T cream cheese
½ t ground ginger

Combine ingredients and whip until smooth and creamy. Serve over Banana-Nut Salad.

Sophisticates often insert into the vagina fruits such as strawberries or cherries (sweet, pitted cherries), or sections of an orange (a seedless orange), or slices of an apple deliciously dipped in honey; thereupon sucking or drawing them out of the vagina again, and eating them with relish. The classical fruit used in this way is the banana ... I have also heard very often of using oysters and mussels in cunnilinctus ... In any case, the practice of inserting any solids into the vagina and sucking them out again should not be attempted by persons with false teeth or a dental plate ...

– G. Legman,
Oragenitalism: Oral Techniques
in Genital Excitation,
(Julian Press, N.Y.), 1969

SOPHISTICATED FRUITS

½ cup dried peaches
½ cup dried pears
½ cup dried apricots
1½ cups cream sherry

Place fruits in 1 qt. jar and pour wine over fruit. Cover and let stand at room temperature for 1 week. Refrigerate until ready to use.

Truly I think a marrow-bone pye, candied eryngoes, preserved dates, or marmalade of cantharides, were much better harbingers; cock-sparrows stew'd, dove's brains, or swan's pizzles, are very provocative; roasted potatoes, or boiled skirrits are your only lofty dishes.

—Thomas Heywood,
The Dumb Knight, *1633*

PRESERVED DATE PIE

1 lb. pitted dates, chopped
2/3 cup water
½ cup chopped nuts

Simmer dates in water until soft. Remove from heat and stir in nuts.

For Crust:

¼ cup soft butter
4 T shortening
1 cup oatmeal
1 cup flour
3/4 t baking soda
3/4 cup brown sugar
1 t vanilla

In large bowl combine ingredients and mix until crumbly. Place half of crumb mixture in well greased pie dish. Spread date filling over crumbs. Cover top with remaining mixture. Bake in 325° oven for 35 minutes. Top with whipped cream or ice cream.

The word papaya *in Cuban Spanish originally referred to the succulent fruit of the* Carica papaya — *and nothing more. In modern times the word has undergone a strange and erotic transformation. Papaya presently refers to the female "fruit," and its use is considered vulgar in polite society. The juicy papaya is now called* fruta bomba *(bomb fruit) by decorous Cubans.*

PAPAYA NECTAR

½ fresh papaya, peeled and seeded
1 oz. lime juice
4 oz. light rum
1 cup crushed ice
  Sugar to taste

Slice papaya into small pieces. Place in blender with remaining ingredients. Blend and serve in chilled cocktail glasses. Serves 2.

The pomegranate is a symbol of fertility and abundance. The Roman encyclopedist, Pliny the Elder, described this delicious fruit as an aphrodisiac. Seeds of the pomegranate are mixed with powdered sugar at Oriental weddings and offered to the guests. When the newlyweds enter their new home pomegranates are broken on the floor, the bursting seeds symbolizing that the marriage will be blessed with many children.

POMEGRANATE HEART MOLD

8 large pomegranates
½ cup sugar
1 T gelatin
4 T cold water

Roll whole unpeeled pomegranates several times with palm of hand to soften fruit. Slice fruit in half and extract juice with reamer. If juice does not equal 2 cups, add water. Pour juice in small pan and add sugar. Heat and stir until sugar is dissolved. Dissolve gelatin in cold water and add to juice mixture. Pour in heart-shaped mold and chill until firm. Top with orange flavored yogurt. Serves 4.

If one desires anothers love, he must take an orange and prick it all over with a needle, then sleep with it under his armpit. If the loved-one then eats the orange, he or she will return love.

— European folklore

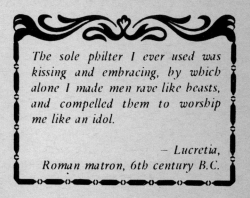

The sole philter I ever used was kissing and embracing, by which alone I made men rave like beasts, and compelled them to worship me like an idol.

— Lucretia,
Roman matron, 6th century B.C.

ORANGE DATE LOAF

1 cup sugar
1 cup shortening
4 eggs, beaten
4 cups flour
1 t soda
1½ cups sour milk
2 T orange rind
1 cup chopped nuts
2 cups chopped dates

Cream sugar and shortening until light and fluffy. Add eggs, flour, nuts, dates and orange rind. Mix soda with sour milk and stir into batter. Pour into greased angel cake pan and bake in 350° oven for 1 hour.

The Spanish conquistadores, *upon arriving in Mexico, noticed that the Aztecs enjoyed a strange green fruit which they called* ahuacatl. *The Indians explained that* ahuacatl *meant "testicle," and was so named because the fruit was capable of exciting intense sexual passion. Thus one of the great treasures of the New World, the avocado, was introduced into Europe. Even today in modern Mexico, the* aguacate *is still considered to be a powerful love stimulant.*

GUACAMOLE AZTECA

2 ripe avocados
1 T orange juice
1 t salt
1½ grated onion
1 green chili, minced
1 tomato, peeled and finely chopped, optional

Peel and mash avocado and combine with remaining ingredients. Use as a dip or with fish, meat or beans.

The avocado or alligator pear frequently appeared on the banquet tables of the licentious 17th century French court. This exotic and erotic fruit was brought from the Echelles of the Levant to fan the fading fires of the aging king, Louis XIV. Louis called the avocado la bonne poire.

COURTLY AVOCADO

1 large avocado
3 T cream cheese
1½ T light cream
1 t mayonnaise
1 t chopped chives
1½ T chopped walnuts
1 T chopped black olives
   Salt to taste
   Lemon juice
   Crisped lettuce leaves
   Grapefruit sections

Cut avocado in half. Remove pit and peel. Extract about 1 T of pulp to enlarge cavity. Mix cheese, cream, mayonnaise, chives, walnuts, olives and salt. Fill cavity with cheese mixture and place halves together. Brush with lemon juice. Wrap and chill for several hours. To serve, cut in thick slices crosswise. Place on lettuce and garnish with grapefruit sections. Serves 2.

In the bawdy houses of 16th century Elizabethan England, prunes were served free of charge to whet the customer's appetite for the more substantial feast to come.

PRUNES ON THE HOUSE

1½ lbs. dried prunes
2 cups powdered sugar, sifted
1 egg white
1 t vanilla
2 t cold water
½ cup finely chopped nuts

Soften prunes in warm water. Drain and dry. Remove pits. Combine sugar, egg, vanilla and water. Beat into stiff paste. Form into small balls and roll in chopped nuts. Stuff prunes with fondant. Stimulus for many.

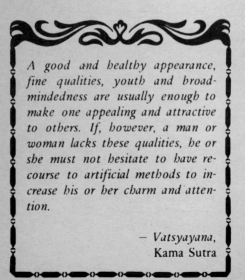

A good and healthy appearance, fine qualities, youth and broad-mindedness are usually enough to make one appealing and attractive to others. If, however, a man or woman lacks these qualities, he or she must not hesitate to have recourse to artificial methods to increase his or her charm and attention.

— Vatsyayana,
Kama Sutra

Eat the white shallots sent from Megara
Or garden herbs that aphrodisiac are,
Or eggs, or honey on Hymettus flowing,
Or nuts upon the sharp-leaved pine-trees growing

– Ovid,
Ars Amatoria, *1st century A.D.*

HUMMUS

2 cups chick peas
½ t soda
1 cup lemon juice
¾ cup sesame oil
4 cloves garlic
2 t salt
2½ T chopped parsley
2 T pine nuts

Cover peas with cold water, add soda and soak overnight. Drain peas and place in kettle with cold water. Simmer for 3 hours or until tender. Drain and press through sieve to make paste. Beat lemon juice and sesame oil until thick. Gradually add to pea paste. Mash garlic with salt and stir into mixture with remaining ingredients. Mix well and place in serving dish. Drizzle oil over top and serve as a spread with meza or sesame crackers. Serve as Hors d'Oeuvres.

Two hazel nuts I threw into the flame,
And to each nut I gave a sweetheart's name.
This with the loudest bounce me sore amazed,
That in a flame of brightest colour blazed.
As blazed the nut so may thy passion grow,
For 'twas thy nut that did so brightly glow.

– John Gay,
Spell, *18th century*

SWEETHEART NUT CUPS

1 cup semi-sweet chocolate chips
3 T butter
  Vanilla ice cream
  Chopped hazel nuts

Melt chocolate and butter in top of double boiler. Place 6 fluted paper cups in muffin pan and line cups with chocolate mixture. Chill. When ready to serve, fill cups with ice cream and sprinkle with nuts. Serves 6.

He who feels that he is weak for coition should drink before going to bed a glassful of very thick honey and eat twenty almonds and one hundred grains of the pine tree. He must follow this regime for three days.

—Shaykh Nefzawi,
The Perfumed Garden,
16th century Arabian love manual

ALMOND PANOCHA

2 cups brown sugar
½ cup light cream
1½ T butter
1 t vanilla
¾ cup chopped toasted almonds

In saucepan combine sugar, cream and butter. Stir constantly until mixture reaches 240° or soft ball stage. Remove from heat. Do not stir. Cool until lukewarm or 110°. Add vanilla and nuts; pour into buttered pan. Cut while warm.

The odor of semen, known as odor aphrodisiacus, *is also found in chestnuts and some thorns.*

– *Dr. Iwan Bloch,*
Odoratus Sexualis, *1933*

FIERY ROASTED NUTS

1 lb. chestnuts
   Dry red wine
¼ cup whipped butter

Cut cross slits on top of chestnuts and lay on flat baking dish. Roast in moderate oven until nuts pop open. Sprinkle with wine and arrange on serving dish. Serve with whipped butter.

BREADS, EGGS & SWEETMEATS

Breads have appeared in erotic cookery mainly because of their association with phallic worship. The worship of the phallus is an age-old practice which flourished in Greece, Rome, India, Bali, the Far East, and among California Indians. The erect and virile male member is its symbol; it is also symbolic of the worship and adoration of man by woman.

The ancient Greek phallic god, Priapus, the son of Aphrodite and Dionysus, was chief diety of Lampsacus of the Hellespont. He is usually pictured with an enormous, erect phallus. Priapus brought luck, protected against thieves, warded off the evil eye, and his grotesque appearance made him the ideal scarecrow in Greek gardens. The Grecian landscape was literally studded with looming phalli, called *olisbokolices*. Every religious Greek faithfully wore his phallic amulet. It was a common practice to bake phallic breads which were eaten at festivals in honor of Priapus. The Romans added the extra dimension of female as well as male loaves of bread to the art of prurient baking.

The custom of phallic baking continued into the early Christian era when these loaves were baked on holy days and carried in religious processions. This practice still continued into the 1820's when, in St. Jean-d'Angley, phallic breads were borne in the feast of Corpus Christi. The church frowned on this erotic custom, and through its influence the breads took on a different form. They came to be baked round, with a cross on top, forevermore known as Hot Cross Buns.

Of all the foods that man has tried in search of sustained sexual vigor, eggs, the organic nuclei of life itself, are by far the most versatile. Eggs are used in the preparation of meats, fish, fowl, vegetables, fruits, drinks, and are the prime ingredients in sweetmeats. But it is the raw egg, sucked clean from the shell, that has the greatest aphrodisiac effect.

The egg is the supreme symbol of fertility, birth and regeneration. Eggs are also said to increase sperm. It is believed that an egg yolk contains the fountain of sexual energy, for it is in the yolk that the spark of life ignites. Eros, the Greek god of love, was said to be born of an egg, and not only did he preside over passion, but fertility as well. Some peoples prefer the egg of one fowl to that of another, but all agree that the egg is an aphrodisiac. The Arabs, the most noted exemplars of erotic egg cookery, recommend the eating of three egg yolks daily for virility. In Algiers egg yolks are mixed with powdered bedbugs. Frenchmen take their egg in cognac, the Americans in beer, while the Persian bride doesn't eat the egg, but throws it against the wall in the hope that her hymen will break as easily.

Whether you like your eggs poached, fried, scrambled, sucked or thrown, you are assured a feast to the palate and a tonic to the spirit.

The modern custom of giving a sweetheart a box of candy as a love offering had its beginnings in the ancient belief of the aphrodisiac properties of sweetmeats. It is no accident that terms of endearment such as "honey", "sugar", and "sweetheart" are heard in love's vocabulary.

Honey is not only one of nature's purest foods, but also one of her most erotic. What man could imagine a more powerful aphrodisiac than that used by lecherous Arabian shiekhs. The nude bodies of beautiful harem girls are painted with honey. Then they are made to run through hashish fields when the potent flowering tops of the plant are heavy with pollen and resin. The shiekhs then lick the sweet intoxicating resin from the girls' bodies until they satiate their wanton appetites. In the Orient, honey is a common substitute for sugar and often appears in love recipes. Chinese honey *(mi tang)* is also used as a binding agent in aphrodisiac pills. Two famous physicians, Galen, a 2nd century Greek, and Avicenna, a 13th century Arab, both highly recommend honey for affairs of the heart.

Two of the world's most cherished flavors, chocolate and vanilla, have considerable erotic repute. The Aztecs were sexually stimulated by chocolate which they drank in honor of Xochiquetzal, the Venus of Aztec mythology. What seems surprising is that the Aztecs, who also knew vanilla, never mixed the two flavors to produce vanilla-flavored chocolate. It was the Europeans, with their refined tastes, who combined the two — and considered both aphrodisiacs. In the 17th century monks were forbidden to eat or drink chocolate lest it tempt them into sins of the flesh. In the licentious French courts chocolates were coated with ambergris in a royal version of the box of candy offering. Vanilla owes its stimulating reputation to the appearance of the bean which

36

resembles the female genitalia. The word "vanilla" is a diminutive of the Latin "vagina."

Sweets are indeed proper fare for the sweetheart, and when given with love have been known to open the body and soul of the receiver.

EGGS, BREADS & SWEETMEATS

How beautiful are thy breasts, my sister, my spouse! thy breasts are more beautiful than wine, and the sweet smell of thy ointments above all aromatical spices.

Thy lips, my spouse, are as dropping honeycomb: honey and milk are under thy tongue; and the smell of thy garments, as the smell of frankincense.

— *Song of Solomon*

HONEY AND MILK

1½ cups milk
½ cup chopped almonds, blanched
½ cup light cream
3 egg yolks
¾ cup honey
¼ t cinnamon
1T cornstarch

Simmer milk and nuts together to boiling. Pour cream, egg yolks, honey and cinnamon in blender and blend until smooth. Dissolve cornstarch in a little cold milk and stir into hot milk. Add egg mixture and stir until thick and creamy. Serves 4.

Breads and cakes baked in the form of the male and female genitalia were very common in ancient Greece and Rome. In Rome they were called coliphia *and* siligones, *and were baked by prostitutes who were referred to as "baker's girls." It was the custom of these prostitutes to entertain their customers in the bake ovens — after they had cooled, of course.*

COLD OVEN BREAD

1 loaf unbaked bread
   Oil or shortening
   Toasted sesame seeds
   Powdered sugar

Slice unbaked bread. Heat a generous amount of oil in skillet and fry bread until brown and crisp. Remove to warm platter and sprinkle with sesame seeds and sugar. (This bread may also be served with honey or syrup.)

The member of Abou el Heiloukh has remained erect
for thirty days without a break, because he did eat onions.
Abou el Heidja has deflowered in one night
Once eighty virgins, and he did not eat or drink between,
Because he surfeited himself first with chick-peas,
And had drunk camel's milk with honey mixed.
Mimoun, the negro, never ceased to spend his sperm,
while he for fifty days without a truce the game was working.
How proud he was to finish such a task!
For ten days more he worked it, not was he yet surfeited,
But all this time he ate but yolk of eggs and bread.

— *Shaykh Nefzawi,*
The Perfumed Garden,
16th century Arabian love manual

MIMOUN'S DELIGHT

3 eggs
3 T milk
6 slices white bread
2 T butter
1 cup honey
¼ t cinnamon
1/8 t nutmeg
1 t anisette liqueur
¼ cup chopped pine nuts

Beat eggs and milk. Dip each bread slice in egg mixture and brown in butter. Place on baking sheet. In saucepan, heat honey, cinnamon, nutmeg and liqueur. Stir until mixture thickens. Spread honey mixture on bread, sprinkle with nuts and place under broiler until syrup bubbles. Serves 6.

Have you done that which certain women are wont to do? They hurl themselves upon their face and with buttocks bared, put bread into their notch and grind it there. When the milling is done they drag out these odorous crumbs and feed them to their husbands in order to fan their love into hotter passion.

— Bishop Burchard of Worms,
De Poenitentia Decretorum,
13th century

CRUMBLY FRIED CHEESE

1 package Camembert cheese
1 egg, beaten
  Bread crumbs
  Oil

Remove rind from cheese and slice into sections. Dip cheese sections in egg, roll in bread crumbs and fry in oil until golden brown. Serve as Hors d'Oeuvres.

Phallic cakes also played a bizarre role in the early history of the church. These cakes, called pinnes (penises) in France, were carried reverently to the church in holy processions during Easter and the feast of Corpus Christi. There the cakes were solemnly blessed by the village priest. In the town of Saintes, Palm Sunday was known as Fete des Pinnes (Feast of the Penises).

PHALLIC COOKIES

1 cup softened butter
1 cup powdered sugar
1 egg, beaten
1½ t vanilla
2½ cups flour, sifted

Cream butter and sugar until light and fluffy. Add egg and mix well. Blend in flour and vanilla. Place dough in pastry tube and form into phallic shapes. Place on lightly buttered cookie sheet and bake in 350° oven for 9 minutes or until lightly browned.

In France, if you are stung by a bee, you have been innoculated with a potent aphrodisiac. But among the Hindus, it is the bee's honey which is nature's elixir and love's nectar.

QUEEN'S PAPAYA

1 papaya
1 cup yogurt
½ cup honey
2 T lemon juice
¼ cup chopped toasted almonds

Peel papaya and slice in half. Remove seeds and fill each half
with yogurt. Combine honey and juice; drizzle over papaya
halves. Sprinkle with nuts. Serves 2.

*A quaint custom among certain lusty medieval German girls
was to frolic naked in wheat before it was ground into flour.
Later the cakes were offered to a beloved who, upon tasting
the delectable morsel, was immediately love-struck and
possessed with a burning desire for the charms of the baker.*

DELECTABLE GERMAN CAKE

½ lb. butter
2½ cups sugar
4 large eggs, separated
1 t lemon juice
1 T grated lemon rind
3 cups flour
3 t baking powder
    Pinch of salt
1 cup milk

Cream butter and sugar until light and fluffy. Beat egg yolks
and add to sugar mixture with lemon juice and rind. Sift dry
ingredients 3 times and add alternately with milk. Beat egg
whites until foamy and fold into batter. Pour into greased and
floured angel cake pan and bake in 325° oven for 1¼ hours.
When cool, sprinkle with powdered sugar.

The origin of the wedding cake comes from the Roman confarreatio, a marriage ceremony in which the bride and groom ate cake made of salt, water and flour. The bride also held three wheat ears, symbols of plenty. In the Middle Ages, the wheat was thrown over the bride, and still later, during the reign of Queen Elizabeth, the wheat was baked into small biscuits made of eggs, milk, sugar, currants and spices. Sesame has always been a popular ingredient in wedding cakes, and harks back to the Greeks who served sesame cakes at wedding banquets as a fructifying influence.

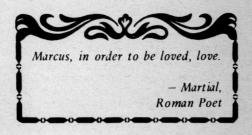

Marcus, in order to be loved, love.

— Martial,
Roman Poet

NUPTIAL NUGGETS

½ lb. softened butter
½ cup powdered sugar
2 cups flour
1 t vanilla
¾ cup chopped walnuts
¼ cup chopped maraschino cherries

Cream butter and sugar until light and fluffy. Blend in flour and vanilla; mix well. Stir in nuts and cherries. Roll dough into small nuggets. Place on buttered cookie sheet and bake in 350° oven for 12 minutes. Dust with additional powdered sugar.

From twelve years old, I oft have been told,
A Pudding it was a delicate bit;
I can Remember my Mother has said,
What a Delight she had to be fed
With a Pudding

Thirteen being past, I longed for to taste,
What Nature or Art could make it so sweet;
For many gay Lasses, about my age,
Perpetually speak on't, that puts me in a rage
For a Pudding

Now at Fifteen, I often have seen,
Most Maids to admire it so;
That their Humor and Pride is to say,
O what a Delight they Have for to play
With a Pudding

— Merry Songs and Ballads, *1893*

PLAYFUL PUDDING

5 slices stale bread, crusts removed
1½ cups milk
1/3 cup sugar
½ cup ground chocolate
3 eggs, separated
1 t vanilla

Slice bread into small cubes. Heat milk, sugar and chocolate and pour over bread. Let stand 10 minutes. Beat egg yolks and vanilla. Pour into bread mixture and beat until smooth. Beat egg whites stiff and fold in carefully. Pour into buttered mold; steam 1 hour. Serve warm with ice cream or hard sauce. Serves 6.

King Louis XIV of France frequently drank alcohol sweetened with sugar to enhance his amatory drive. Hence, wedding couples of the period ate cakes dipped in alcohol to insure a nuptial night of naughty delight.

CINNAMON RUM BALLS

2 cups graham cracker crumbs
2 T cocoa
1 t cinnamon
1 t grated orange rind
1/8 t salt
1 cup sifted powdered sugar
1/3 cup light rum

Mix all ingredients and form into balls. Roll balls in additional powdered sugar. Place in air tight container and let sit in cool place for 10 days. Serve.

M. de Sade gave a ball, to which he invited a numerous company: a splendid supper was served at midnight: now the marquis had mixed with the dessert a profusion of chocolate, flavoured with vanilla which was found delicious, and of which everybody freely partook. All at once the guests, both men and women, were seized with a burning sensation of lustful ardour; the cavaliers attacked the ladies without any concealment. The essence of cantharides circulating in their veins left them neither modesty nor reserve in their imperious pleasures; excess was carried to the most fatal extremity; pleasure became murderous; blood flowed upon the floor, and the women only smiled at the horrible effects of their uterine rage . . .

> – Moreau of Tours,
> *describing the effcts of*
> *cantharides at a dinner given*
> *by the Marquis de Sade*

CHOCOLATE BLANC MANGE

4 cups milk
3 oz. unsweetened chocolate, cut in small pieces
4 T cornstarch
¾ cup sugar
¼ t salt
1 t vanilla
   Sweetened whipped cream
   Chopped toasted almonds

Heat milk, add chocolate and stir over low heat until chocolate dissolves. Mix cornstarch, sugar and salt with a little cold milk and stir into chocolate mixture. Cook over low heat until sauce is smooth and thickened. Pour sauce in top of double boiler and cook over hot water for 20 minutes (do not boil water). Remove from heat, add vanilla and pour into oiled mold. Chill until set. Unmold and serve with whipped cream and chopped almonds. Serves 6.

Duck Eggs are superior to the Hen as are Pigeon Eggs superior to the Duck. The Sparrow gives the greatest egg of them all.

– Anon,
– Lucayos [Bahamas] Cook Book, 1660

HOT EGGS

4 eggs
4 T chili sauce
2 strips bacon, halved

Break eggs in buttered baking dish. Top each egg with 1 T chili sauce and half strip of bacon. Bake in 400° oven until eggs are set and bacon is crisp. Serves 2.

PARIS (WNS) — German men have given up sending chocolates when they get sweet on a girl.

Instead they are giving the girls sticks of licorice. Sales of licorice have shot up as the girls lick away at the sticks.

The reason: they claim licorice makes them feel "sexy."

West German scientists have been probing the new fad after reports that hundreds of German girls on holiday at coastal resorts were eating licorice instead of ice cream. They confirm that licorice contains traces of estrogen.

— San Francisco Examiner, *1969*

ANISE COOKIES

1¼ cups butter
2 cups sugar
4 eggs, lightly beaten
2 cups ground almonds
2 t vanilla
2 T anise seed
2 t baking powder
½ t salt
6 cups flour

Cream butter and sugar until light and fluffy; stir in eggs. Add almonds, vanilla and anise seed. Sift dry ingredients and stir into butter mixture. Roll into balls and flatten on greased baking sheet with back of spoon. Bake in 350° oven for 30 minutes or until cookies are very light brown.

He will fry a good number of eggs in fresh fat and butter and, when they are well cooked, he will mix them with honey. If he will eat as much as possible of this with a piece of bread, he will be able to soothe and comfort all through the night . . .

— *Shaykh Nefzawi,*
The Perfumed Garden,
16th century Arabian love manual

LIGHTLY FRIED EGGS

2 T butter
1 T finely chopped green onion
2 T diced cooked ham
4 eggs
    Salt and pepper to taste

Melt butter in heavy skillet; add onion and ham. Cook until onions are soft. Break eggs into dish and carefully slide into skillet. Dust with salt and pepper. Part of onion mixture will cook into eggs. Serve remainder as a garnish. Serves 4.

Virtually all peoples, ancient and modern, primitive and civilized, have used and praised alcohol as an aphrodisiac *par excellence.* The maidens of antiquity were seduced with mead, the earliest alcoholic beverage known to man. A sweet wine made from fermented honey, mead was called *balche* by the Mayan Indians of Mexico, and retained its popularity in Europe until the beginning of the 18th century. The mysterious nectar and ambrosia, known as "wine of the gods," stimulated the Greek dieties on Mt. Olympus in their frequent wild escapades. The Greeks were so enamored of wine that they created a god, Dionysus, to preside over the grape and the orgiastic religious rites accompanying its use. Later the Romans borrowed Dionysus, changed his name to Bacchus, and continued in grand style the tradition of holding druken feasts in his honor. These Bacchanalian orgies were attended by voluptuous *bacchantes,* female devotees of Bacchus who lent their lusty charms to the revelry of the occasion.

Around 800 A.D., Jabir ibn Hayyan, an Arab to whom mankind is profoundly indebted, developed the technique of distillation. True to the spirit of scientific inquiry, ibn Hayyan was attempting to discover the "spirit" in wine responsible for its intoxicating power. He called the substance he distilled from wine *alkuhul,* meaning "finely refined spirit," after a fine antimony powder used for painting the eyelids. In medieval Europe, alcohol was called *aqua ardens,* or "ardent spirits." The aging king, Louis XIV, had tonics specially made to awaken his slumbering amatory spirits. These tonics, made with brandy, sugar and essences, were the first *potions cordiales* and *liqueurs.* Some other aphrodisiac beverages of renown are elecampane, a flowerseed concoction, vervain, a drink made from mistletoe berries, and *tanto krin,* a Russian brew composed of alcoholic brine and powdered reindeer antlers.

Whether the spirit is brew, demon rum or malmsey, a wine drunk by medieval witches to "excite them to venery," alcohol taken in moderation truly makes the heart grow fonder. Booze has amatory effects on both the spirit and the flesh. Psychologically, alcohol lowers inhibitions, leaving one guilt-free and unresisting to seduction. Physiologically, the blood vessels become dilated, the skin radiates warmth, blood gorges the genitalia, and a tingling sensation ensues. Accompanied with fine cuisine, soft lights and romantic music, this warm, alcohol-induced glow has led straight to the boudoir. "Eat, drink, and be merry!" is more than just a saying; it's a promise. Keep in mind, however, that the secret to affairs of the cup is *moderation*. Heed the words of the Bard in *Macbeth*:

MACDUFF: What three things does drink especially provoke?
PORTER: Marry, sir, nose-painting, sleep, and urine. Lechery, sir, it provokes and it unprovokes; it provokes the desire, but it takes away the performance . . .

Whenever I take wine I have to think
Of Venus, for as cold engenders hail
A lecherous mouth begets a lecherous tail
A woman in her cups has no defense,
As lechers know from long experience.

– Chaucer,
Canterbury Tales, *1478*

DANDELION WINE
2½ qts. dandelion flowers
4 qts. hot water
4 lemons, sliced
2 oranges, sliced
3 lbs. sugar
2 t granulated yeast

Remove stems from flowers. Place in crock, pour hot water over flowers and let stand for 3 days. Strain. Dissolve yeast in small amount of cold water. Add dandelion water, yeast solution, lemons, oranges and sugar. Cover crock and set in cool dark place. Wine is ready to decant when you can hear it working, about 3 weeks. Strain before decanting. Yields 4 quarts.

O master of ours, the negro knows no other passions than for coition and good wine. He keeps making love night and day, and his member rests only when he himself is asleep.

What does he live upon?

Upon yolks of eggs fried in fat and swimming in honey, and upon white bread; he drinks nothing but old muscatel wine.

— Shaykh Nefzawi,
The Perfumed Garden,
16th century Arabian love manual

PASSION PUNCH

2 cups muscatel wine
½ cup brandy
1 qt. milk
1 cup heavy cream
   Sugar to taste
   Nutmeg

In punch bowl combine spirits, milk, cream and sugar. Sprinkle with nutmeg and serve at room temperature. Serves 6.

Take 4 gallons & a half of water, six pound and a half of honey, a pound and a half of ston'd raisons, a race of ginger, boyle all these together two houres scumming it all ye while. Then pour it into an earthen vessell and when it is almost cold put in a small bitt of brown bread toasted and spread over with yeast. Lett it stand covered two days. Then do it up, and hang into your vessell an ounce of coriander seed bruised and the peel of a fresh lemmon. When it has done working stop it close and cottle it in 3 weeks.

— Mead recipe,
Lucayos Cook Book, *1660*

BEER OF BAWDY BOB

5 gals. tepid water
3 lbs. sugar
1 can hop flavored malt
1 package yeast

In 6 gal. crock, place sugar, malt and water. Stir until sugar and malt dissolve. Dissolve yeast in 1 glass tepid water and pour into sugar mixture. Cover with light cloth. Skim foam off brew twice daily. Beer will brew best if a constant 70° temperature is maintained. Bottle and cap brew after 4 full days, adding 1 t sugar to each quart before filling. Yields 20 quarts.

Have you done that which certain women are accustomed to do? They save their menstrual blood, mix it into the food and drink which they give their husbands, in order that their husbands may love them more ardently. If you have done that you should do penance for five years on the legal holidays.

— *Bishop Burchard of Worms,*
De Poenitentia Decretorum,
13th century

BLOODY MARIA

1 jigger tequila
4 oz. tomato juice
1/3 jigger lemon juice
   Dash of Worcestershire
   Dash of chili powder
   Salt to taste

Combine ingredients in tall glass with ice cubes. Muddle well.
Serves 1.

*The milk of a white cow who has a white calf nestling beside
her possesses excellent [aphrodisiac] properties, and, if drunk,
lengthens one's life and brings fame and fortune.*

> — *Vatsyayana*,
> Kama Sutra,
> *4th century Hindu love manual*

STIMULATING CHOCOLATE RUM

2 squares unsweetened chocolate
2/3 cup sugar
½ t cinnamon
   Pinch of salt
½ cup water
2 qts. extra rich milk
   Rum

In saucepan combine chocolate, sugar, cinnamon, salt and
water. Stir until chocolate melts. Add milk and heat to boiling.
Pour 1 jigger of rum into each cup and fill with chocolate
mixture. Serves 8.

Alcohol is the chief sexual stimulant among drinks.

— *Th. H. Van de Velde, M.D.*,
Ideal Marriage, *1928*

APRICOT CORDIAL

2 fifths vodka
2 lbs. dried apricots
2 lbs. rock candy, broken in small pieces

Place all ingredients in stone crock. Cover and stir daily. After 3 weeks, strain and decant. Yields 2 fifths.

In two pints Chablis, crush one ounce each of vanilla beans, cinnamon sticks, dried rhubarb, and mandrake or ginseng. Let stand for two weeks, stirring daily. Strain through cheesecloth; add amber. Bottle. Use as an aphrodisiac.

— *Classic French love wine*

VIN APHRODISIAQUE

4 cups Chablis
1 cup sherry
½ cup brandy
2 cups water
1 cup sugar
3 lemons, sliced

In large pitcher combine sugar and water. Stir until sugar is thoroughly dissolved. Add wine, brandy and lemon slices. Chill well and serve over ice in large cocktail glasses. Garnish each glass with lemon slice. Serves 4.

A loaf of bread,
A jug of wine
  And thou, beneath the bough,
Were paradise enow.

– *Omar Khayyam,*
Rubaiyat, *11th century*

RUBAIYAT RED

2 glasses port
8 drops curacao
2 thin lemon slices, studded with
2 cloves

In cocktail pitcher mix port and curacao. Pour in wine glasses. Add lemon slices. Serves 2.

Put into your stands 45 gallons of boiling water. Stir in one and one half bushels of Corn meal let it stand 20 minuts Stir well let it stand 20 minuts put in 2 gallons of Cold water Stir well and put in 6 quarts of malt let it stand 20 minuts Stir in one half bushel of bran let it stand 1 hour Stir every 15 minutes until Cool enough to Cool off.

–Samuel Sneed,
Corn liquor recipe,
North Carolina, 1831

MOUNTAIN DEW FIZZ

½ pt. corn whiskey
1 cup light cream
2 egg whites
1 T grenadine
2 T sugar
  Soda water

Combine whiskey, cream, egg whites, grenadine and sugar in electric blender. Blend until smooth and creamy. Fill cocktail glasses half full. Add ice and fill with soda water. Serves 4.

A ... very heady flavor is given to the vulva ... by the application of sweet still wines, such as a good Port, Muscatel, or Malaga.

– G. Legman,
Oragenitalism: Oral Techniques
in Genital Excitation,
(Julian Press, N.Y.), 1969

HEADY PORT WINE

1 qt. grape juice
2 lbs. sugar
2 cups raisins
2 qts. water
1 yeast cake

Mix all ingredients in stone crock and cover. Stir mixture twice a week. After 2 weeks, strain mixture through cheese cloth and squeeze well. Decant and let stand for 30 days before drinking. Yields 3 quarts.

Take of amber, half a drachm; musk, two scruples, aloes, one drachm and a half; pound them all together, pour upon the mass a sufficient quantity of spirits of wine so that the liquor may cover it to the height of about five fingers' breadth; expose it to sand heat, filter and distil it, close it hermetically, and administer it in broth in the dose of 3 or 5 drops. This liquor is also advantageous when mixed with syrup, prepared as follows: – Take of cinnamon water, 4 oz: orange and rose water, each 6 oz, and sugar candy.

– *16th century French love recipe*

VIN de l' AMOUR

1 qt. sherry
2 T sugar
   Juice of 1 orange
½ t orange rind
1 t vanilla
½ t cinnamon

In saucepan combine ingredients and heat to boiling. Serve hot in mugs. Serves 8.

There is a devil in every berry of the grape.

– Koran

DEVIL BERRY FLIP

1 6 oz. can frozen pink lemonade
1½ cups Rosé wine
½ cup sliced strawberries
½ cup crushed ice

Combine ingredients in electric blender and blend until smooth and foamy. Serves 4.

Chicha is a native drink that has been brewed for over five hundred years from Mexico to South America. Among the Cuna Indians of the San Blas archipelago, chicha is only drunk during female puberty rites (inna). At the end of the fourth day of inna the girl's hair is cut very short and she is given a formal name (musway). She is now ready for marriage. The women of the tribe make corn chicha by masticating the kernels and letting the masa ferment for three days. The Cuna believe that the fermentation of chicha is an act of God.

GALLO Y CHICHA DE MILAGRA

1 6 lb. rooster or stewing hen,
     cut in large pieces
3½ qts. chicha
3 onions, chopped
8 tomatoes, cleaned and peeled
1½ cups white wine
1 cup vinegar
½ cup butter
1½ cups beer
4 oz. Mexican chocolate
2 chorizo sausages, sliced in large chunks
1 large cauliflower, broken
8 carrots, cut in large pieces
8 potatoes, cut in large pieces
1 cup raisins
25 prunes
1 3½ oz. jar capers, drained
1½ cups cooked chick peas
1 cup green olives, with pits
2 t Tabasco
12 pumpkin seeds
2 cloves garlic
3 bay leaves
½ t nutmeg
½ t poppy seeds
1½ T sesame seeds
2 t salt
8 peppercorns

Pour chicha in large kettle. Add rooster and onions and marinate 8 to 10 hours. In small skillet toast spices, seeds and garlic until lightly browned. Place in blender with tomatoes and wine. Blend thoroughly. Pour mixture into kettle. Add vinegar, butter, beer, chocolate and Tabasco. Simmer over low heat for 4 hours. Add cauliflower, carrots, potatoes, raisins, prunes, chorizo, capers, chick peas and olives. Simmer until vegetables are tender. Serve in soup plates over hot white rice. Serves 10.

CHICHA DE ARTIGA

1 large pineapple
1 apple, unpeeled and quartered
1 cup seedless grapes
1½ lbs. dark brown sugar
6 cloves
½ t nutmeg
1 cinnamon stick
3½ qts. water

Quarter pineapple and peel, leaving ½ inch of pulp on skin. Place skin in large crock or clay pot. Add remaining ingredients, mashing grapes between fingers. Stir until sugar is dissolved. Cover and let stand 1 week. Strain. Chicha may be served as a drink over cracked ice with a garnish of lime. Yields 3½ quarts.

Rose wine you will make like this: Thread together rose-leaves from which the white part has been removed, and steep as many as possible in wine for seven days. After seven days take the rose-leaves out of the wine, and in the same way put in other fresh rose-leaves threaded together, to rest seven days in the wine, then take them out. Repeat a third time, take out the rose-leaves, strain the wine, and, when you want to use it for drinking, add honey to make rose wine. But take care to use the best rose-leaves, when the dew has dried off them. Make violet wine the same way as above, and mix with honey in the same way.

– Apicius,
3rd century Roman aphrodisiac
Rose Wine Recipe,
The Roman Cookery Book,
(George G. Harrap & Co., London),
1958

SATURNALIA CAKES

½ lb. butter
4 cups sifted flour
3 cups sugar
1 t cinnamon
½ cup white wine
½ cup rose petal wine
6 eggs, beaten
   Oil
   Powdered sugar

Cut butter into flour; add sugar and cinnamon. Add wines and eggs. If dough is too soft for rolling, gradually add more sifted flour. Roll dough into thick sheet and cut into strips. Form strips into figure eights. Fry in hot oil. Drain and dust with powdered sugar. (Rose water may be substituted for rose wine.)

Three things to ruin monks combine —
Venery, gluttony, and wine.

— Ducange,
Glossaire

FLAN DEL DIABLO

6 egg yolks
6 T sugar
   Pinch of salt
6 T sherry

Combine egg yolks, sugar and salt in double boiler. Beat mixture until thick and lemon colored. Gradually beat in sherry. Place over hot, but not boiling water and beat until thick and fluffy (4 to 6 minutes). Remove from heat and serve immediately. Serves 4.

Alcohol taken in moderation will temporarily inhibit inhibitions and reduce anxiety, therefore acting as a sex stimulant.

– Dr. Albert Ellis, 1960

DEMON RUM FLUFF

3 T butter
3 T flour
1 cup warm milk
½ cup sugar
Pinch of salt
4 eggs, separated
Rum

Melt butter and blend in flour. Add milk and stir until sauce thickens. Beat egg yolks with sugar and salt. Add beaten yolks and 3 T rum to white sauce. Beat egg whites until stiff and fold into mixture. Pour into buttered casserole. Place casserole in pan of warm water and bake in 300° oven for 35 minutes. Before serving, pour 3 oz. rum over top and serve immediately. Serves 4.

Wine was the most popular table drink among the city dwellers of Rome and Byzantium, whereas highly spiced beer was the favorite of the rural peasants. The Roman love of champagne was carried to fantastic extremes. Men and women of Imperial Rome would gather at the balnea mixta *(mixed bath), shed their togas, and leap with unabandoned glee into bubbly pools of champagne.*

FRUITS BATHED IN CHAMPAGNE

1 cup sliced fresh strawberries
1 cup sliced fresh pineapple
   Powdered sugar to taste
1 oz. brandy
2 cups chilled champagne
2 fresh mint sprigs

Place well chilled fruit in individual compotes. Sprinkle with powdered sugar and pour brandy over fruit. Fill compote with champagne and garnish with mint sprig. Serves 2.

Food and drink are, further, powerful sexual stimulants. This is true even of the simplest and most wholesome nourishment, but it is more especially true of flesh meat, and, above all, of alcohol in its stronger forms such as spirits, liqueurs, sparkling and heavy wines, and even many English beers.

                    – Havelock Ellis,
Studies in the Psychology of Sex, 1920

TEMPTING TRIFLE

12 lady fingers
½ cup blackberry jam
2 oz. brandy
2 oz. cointreau
3 cups vanilla custard or pudding
    Whipped cream
    Blanched almonds

Split lady fingers and spread with jam. Place halves together and lay in bottom of deep dish. Pour over brandy and cointreau and let soak 30 minutes. Pour cool custard over lady fingers. Top with whipped cream and almonds. Serves 6.

> *Alcohol liberates existing desires that are normally held in check ... usually prolonging the erection and deferring climax at .10 to .15 blood alcohol level.*
>
> — Leon D. Adams,
> Commonsense Book of Drinking,
> 1960

dam-i-an'a, n. *[L., origin uncertain.] In medicine, a drug composed of the leaves of Mexican plants of the genus* Turnera; *used as an aphrodisiac, or tonic.*

— Webster's Twentieth
Century Dictionary

DAMIANA FIZZ

1 cup crushed ice
1 oz. lemon juice
1 oz. sweet lime juice
1 T powdered sugar
4 oz. half and half
2 egg whites
4 oz. Damiana

Combine all ingredients in blender. Cover and blend until smooth and creamy. Serves 4.

SOUPS & POTIONS

Love potions, conjured from witches' cauldrons and sorceresses' incantations, have been brewed for lovers for centuries. They are among the most diabolic of aphrodisiacs. Usually they were composed of horrific substances; the more disgusting the potion, the more powerful its effect.

Aphrodisiac philtres were concocted by the ancients of Assyria, Egypt, Persia and China, although the greatest adepts were the Greek women of Thessaly. Thessaly was the home of magic and the cult of the arch-sorceress Medea. In his play, *Medea,* Seneca, the Roman dramatist, portrays the sorceress sprinkling herbs by moonlight, "With venom extracted from serpents, entrails and organs of unclean birds, the heart of a screech owl, and vampire's vitals, ripped from living flesh . . . All the while murmuring her magic into her piltres." And Horace, in his *Epodes,* describes an equally appalling love potion prepared from wild fig growing on a tomb, bones and feathers of a screech owl (a prime ingredient), and bones snatched from the mouth of a hungry bitch. But the most famous ancient ingredient was *hippomanes,* a small piece of flesh taken from the forehead of a new foaled colt. *Hippomanes* was especially effective when reduced to a powder and mixed with a loved one's blood. Caesonia, wife of Caligula, gave the Roman emperor a love potion of *hippomanes* which made "The boiling blood [run] hissing through his veins, Till the mad vapor mounted to his brains."

The Latin word for philtre, *venenum,* is the same as for poison. The 1st century Roman poet, Lucretius, came to an early end in his forty-third year, driven to insanity and suicide by the effects of a love potion. The situation became so outrageous that the Romans drove the philtre brewers from the market place. The Senate forbade the dispensing of philtres under threat of severe penalties. Later Venetian law also considered the compounding of love potions highly criminal, and in modern America it is illegal to administer a philtre.

Fetishism, which is related to sympathetic magic, also provided some of the bizarre ingredients of love potions. Hair (preferably pubic), nails, skin, sweat and bones, as well as bits and scraps of a loved one's clothing were either burnt to ashes and secreted in soups and drinks, or worn as love charms and amulets. Cow dung was a favorite component in the aphrodisiac brews of the Navajo Indians, while the Apaches favored human excrement. The Cree Indians of Canada were most noted for their love charms and potions. Other favorite ingredients were virile semen and menstrual blood, which isn't surprising considering their high hormone content.

During the Middle Ages, when witchcraft was rampant in Europe, the Italians were famous for their philtres. During this period the alchemists added their contribution to the thriving love potion trade. Potable metals and precious stones, the more costly being the most potent, were sold for extravagant sums. Tincture of gold was a luxurious favorite. Cleopatra, that royal wench of whom the Bard has written: "Age cannot wither her, nor custom stale her infinite variety . . ." is known to have drunk pearls dissolved in vinegar.

The scarcity of such exotic items as flesh of brigand and blood of blind infant eventually led the love starved masses to experiment with more conventional ingredients, especially those foods then considered aphrodisiacs. All the elements of the witches' craft were still present; the murmured incantations, the bubbling cauldron, the magical herbs and spices.

In 14th century Europe a popular soup for husbands and lovers was prepared with beans and cock's testicles. Fennel and coriander soups were highly esteemed in the Mediterranean countries. Among the Orientals, seafood soups were considered highly efficacious. Crayfish, shark's fin and eel soup would inflame the passions of the most unyielding paramour, but the strongest of them all was bird's nest soup. Made from the nests of sea swallows, this provocative soup is composed of edible seaweed glued together by the swallow's saliva and the spawn of small fish, and is the classical example of Oriental culinary seduction.

If you are ever seduced by a love potion, take solace in the fact that in most places, including the American Ozarks, the victim of a philtre or love charm is not held morally responsible for his or her actions. Satan is the villain, and love the rogue.

Pound the shell of a male venus's comb (a mollusk) to a very fine powder, add some urine, and let stand for three days, after which time put it out at noon to dry in the sun. Then dip this in donkey-water and allow it to steep another three days. Again let it dry in the noonday sun and then sprinkle it lightly with the dew of flower blossoms; this will disperse the odor of the urine. Drink from the solution at the time of copulation and you will be endowed with extraordinary potency.

– Ancient Chinese love potion

BIRD'S NEST SOUP

¼ lb. bird's nest
2 small chicken breasts
4 cups water
¼ cup sliced Chinese dried mushrooms
2 T diced cooked ham
1 T chopped parsley
   Salt to taste
1 T corn starch

Soak bird's nest for 1 hour in cold water. Cook chicken breasts in water until tender. Remove chicken; bone and dice. Add bird's nest to chicken stock and simmer for 30 minutes. Soak mushrooms in cold water for 20 minutes. Add chicken, mushrooms, ham, parsley and salt to stock and cook 5 minutes longer. Dissolve corn starch in 3 T water and add to soup. Stir until soup thickens. Serves 4.

Boil shark fins (Sha ch'i) in water over a period of several days, boiling for one hour per day, until meat is pure white and skin peels off at a touch. Eat and await love's call.

– Ancient Chinese
shark fin love recipe

SHARK FIN SOUP

¼ lb. prepared shark fin
1 onion
5 thin slices ginger root
3 lbs. chicken wings
1¼ qts. water
1 T sesame oil
2 green onions
1 T dry sherry
½ cup julienne bamboo shoots
1½ t soy sauce
½ t salt
1 T corn starch

Soak shark fin in cold water overnight. Rinse well under cold water. In large kettle place fins with water, ½ onion and 3 slices ginger. Bring to a boil and cook for 2½ hours. Drain and cut fins into small pieces. Cook chicken in additional 1¼ qts. water with remaining onion and 2 slices of ginger for 1 hour. Strain and reserve broth. Bone chicken and add to broth with fins. Heat oil in saucepan. Mince remaining ginger and green onion. Saute slowly for 4 minutes. Add to broth with sherry and bamboo shoots. Bring broth to a boil. In small amount of cold water mix soy sauce, cornstarch and salt. Pour into soup and stir until thickened. Serves 6.

The tortoise, like the ram, goat, ox, elephant, ass, serpent and fish, was an object of pious veneration among the ancients. The statue of the celestial Venus stands with one foot on a tortoise, which was sacred to her. The head of the tortoise represents, by the extended head and neck, the virile male member. For this reason tortoise soup is considered a potent aphrodisiac.

TURTLE SOUP

4 cups prepared green turtle soup
2 T tomato puree
½ cup dry sherry
   Salt and pepper to taste

Combine soup and tomato puree and heat to boiling. Remove
from heat, stir in sherry and season to taste. Serves 4.

*Aware that her youth was passing and wishing to oust all the
rest of her decrepit lover's women, she took pains to enthrall
him by the use of magic plants.*

*At the same time she re-awakened his juvenile ardour by the
judicious use of fish soup, milk, liquified butter, garlic, onions,
and the other virile adjuvants.*

—Kshemendra,
Samayamatrika

CRAYFISH SOUP

2 small onions, chopped
½ cup chopped celery
2 cloves garlic, minced
½ cup olive oil
2 tomatoes, peeled and chopped
3 T chopped parsley
10 peppercorns
1 bay leaf
   Pinch of saffron
3 lbs. unboned white fish, cut in chunks
½ cup dry white wine
6 cups cold water
24 crayfish

Saute onion, celery and garlic in oil until soft. Add tomatoes, seasonings, fish, wine and water. Boil rapidly for 10 minutes. Strain and return stock to kettle; bring to boil. Clean crayfish and drop immediately into boiling stock. Cover and simmer until crayfish turns red, about 10 minutes. Serves 4.

To make oneself beloved there shall be taken, to wit, the heart of a dove, the liver of a sparrow, the womb of a swallow, the kidney of a hare, and they shall be reduced to impalpable powder. Then the person who shall compound the philtre shall add an equal part of his own blood, dried and in the same way powdered. If the person whom it is desired to draw into love is caused to swallow this powder in a dose of two or three drachms marvellous success will follow.

– Pierre Mora,
Zekerboni

BROTH SUPREME

2 cups chicken broth
1½ cups water
1¾ cups clear clam broth
2 T sherry
1 small avocado, sliced
   Whipped cream
1½ t finely minced parsley
   Paprika

Heat broths and water to boiling. Remove from heat and add sherry. Place 3 thick slices of avocado in each soup dish, pour soup over avocado and top with whipped cream, parsley and paprika. Serves 4.

Fillet of fenny snake,
In the cauldron boil and bake;
Eye of newt and toe of frog,
Wool of bat and tongue of dog,
Adder's fork and blind-worm's sting,
Lizard's leg and howlet's wing,

Scale of dragon, tooth of wolf,
Witches' mummy, maw and gulf
Of the ravin'd salt-sea shark,
Root of hemlock digged i ' the dark,
Liver of blaspheming Jew,
Gall of goat and slips of yew
Sliver'd in the moon's eclipse,
Nose of Turk and Tartar's lips,
Finger of birth-strangled babe
Ditch-deliver'd by a drab,

Cool it with a baboon's blood,
Then the charm is firm and food.

—Shakespeare,
Macbeth, *1606*

LECHER'S LENTIL SOUP

1½ cups dry lentils
6 slices bacon, chopped
1 large onion, chopped
1 clove garlic, chopped
1 lb. soup beef
3 large carrots, chopped
6 stalks celery, chopped
2 bay leaves
2 t salt
8 cups cold water
1 cup tomato sauce
1 16 oz. can tomatoes, chopped
1½ cups chopped cabbage

In large kettle saute bacon, onion and garlic until lightly browned. Add lentils, beef, carrots, celery, bay leaves, salt and water. Simmer for 1½ hours. Remove meat, chop fine, and return to soup. Add tomato sauce, tomatoes and cabbage. Simmer for 30 minutes longer. If soup is too thick, add more water as necessary. Serves 8.

To increase Ye Powers. *Take a Cock-Sparrow and Pluck it whilst living, then throw it to ten wasps who will sting it to death. Add the Intestines of a Black Raven and Oil of Lilac plus Chamomile. Cook all in Beef-Fat until the flesh is in shreds. Put into a bottle and hold near for use. Ye shall see* Marvels.

— Lucayos Cook Book, 1660

Straight to the 'pothecary's shop I went,
And in love powder all my money spent;
Behap what will, next Sunday after prayers,
When to the alehouse Lubberkin repairs,
These golden flies into his mug I'll throw,
And soon the swain with fervent love shall glow.

– John Gay,
Shepherd's Week, *1714*

CHILLED SUNDAY SOUP

3 cups tomato juice
¼ cup finely minced celery
2 radishes, sliced paper thin
3 green onions, chopped
   Tabasco sauce
   Smoke flavored salt

Chill tomato juice. Before serving, add celery and radishes.
Garnish with onions. Pass Tabasco and smoke flavored salt.
Serves 4.

If thou wilt that a woman bee not visious nor desire men, take
the private members of a Woolfe, and the haires which doe
grow on the cheekes or eyebrowes of him, and the haires
which bee under his beard, and burne it all, and give it to her
to drinke, when she knoweth not, and she shal desire no other
man.

– Albertus Magnus,
Book of the Marvels of the World,
13th century

CELERY SOUP

1½ cups chopped celery
3 T minced onion
1½ cups consomme
4 T butter
6 T flour
3 cups milk
1 t salt
½ t paprika
   Shredded chipped beef

Simmer celery and onions in consomme until tender. Melt butter and blend in flour, salt and paprika. Add slowly to consomme mixture. Stir in milk and heat to boiling. Pour into bouillon cups and garnish with shredded chipped beef. Serves 6.

Canidia crown'd with wreathing snakes
Dishevell'd, thus the silence breaks,
"Now the magic fire prepare,
And from graves, uprooted tear
Trees, whose horrors gloomy spread
Round the mansions of the dead,
Bring the eggs and plumage foul
Of a midnight shrieking owl,
Be they will besmear'd with blood
Of the blackest venom'd toad,
Bring the choicest drugs of Spain,
Produce of the poisonous plain,
Then into the charm be thrown,
Snatch'd from famish'd bitch, a bone,
Burn them all with magic flame,
Kindled first by Colchian dame.

— Horace,
describing a love potion made by
the witch Canidia, 1st century B.C.

COCK-A-LEEKIE

1 large stewing hen, cut up
4 cups water
4 cups beef or veal stock
12 leeks, white part only, sliced
1 bay leaf
2 t salt
¼ t white pepper
2 T chopped parsley
¼ cup rice
12 prunes, optional

In large kettle, place hen, water, stock, half of leeks, bay leaf, salt and pepper. Simmer for 3 hours. Skim off fat, strain broth and bone chicken. Return chicken and broth to kettle. Add remaining leeks, parsley, rice and prunes. Simmer for 30 minutes. Serves 8.

I shall show you a love philtre, without medicaments, without herbs, without a witch's incantations. It is this: If you want to be loved, love.

— Seneca,
Epistles, *1st century A.D.*

ALMOND SOUP ASARTE

½ cup blanched almonds
1 cup white chicken meat, cooked
2½ cups chicken broth
¼ cup dry white wine
1 cup cream
½ t dry mustard
   Salt and white pepper to taste
   Chopped parsley

Grind almonds and chicken meat. Place in double boiler with remaining ingredients. Simmer slowly for 1 hour. Garnish with parsley. Serves 4.

Roast hummingbird hearts, then grind them into a powder.
Sprinkle beloved with powder and await amorous results.

— Louisiana Creole love recipe

CREOLE FILE GUMBO

1 large chicken breast
1½ cups water
1 small onion, chopped
1 clove garlic, minced
1 small green pepper, chopped
2 T bacon drippings
3 tomatoes, peeled and chopped
½ lb. fresh okra, sliced
¾ lb. cooked shrimp
¾ lb. crab meat
    Salt and pepper to taste
1 t filé powder

Simmer chicken in water until tender. Bone chicken and set aside. Saute onion, garlic and pepper in drippings until soft. Stir in tomatoes and simmer for 5 minutes; add to chicken broth. Add okra and cook over low heat for 1 hour or until okra is tender. Place chicken, shrimp, crab, salt and pepper in broth and simmer for 15 minutes. Remove from heat and stir in filé powder. Serves 4.

I didn't know if it was day or night
I started kissing everything in sight
But when I kissed the cop down at 34th and Vine
He broke my little bottle of Love Potion Number Nine.

— American song,
Love Potion Number Nine

PEPPER POT POTION

1 small onion, chopped
1 small green pepper, chopped
½ cup chopped celery
2 T bacon drippings
3 T flour
4 cups chicken broth
1 cup tomato sauce
2 tomatoes, peeled and chopped
½ lb. cooked honeycomb tripe, sliced
½ cup rice
1 t celery salt
½ t white pepper

Saute onion, pepper and celery in drippings until soft. Stir in flour. Add remaining ingredients and simmer for 1 hour. Serves 6.

Rinasce piu gloriosa! *(It rises more gloriously than ever!)*

> *— Italian saying about the effects of broad bean soup*

BROAD BEAN SOUP

½ lb. broad beans
1 small onion, chopped
¾ cup chopped celery
1 clove garlic, minced
2½ qts. water
2 large tomatoes, peeled and chopped
2 T olive oil
1 t oregano
    Salt and pepper to taste

In large kettle place beans, onions, celery, garlic and water. Cover and simmer over low heat for 1½ hours or until beans are tender. Saute tomato, oregano, salt and pepper in olive oil for 5 minutes. Add to soup and cook for 15 minutes longer. Serves 8.

Mix together black dust from a tomb, venom of a toad, flesh of a brigand, lung of an ass, blood of a blind infant, bile of an ox and flesh of corpses rifled from graves.

SALEM PEA SOUP

2 cups dry split peas
1½ lbs. ham hocks
3 qts. water
2 carrots, grated
2 small onions, minced
1 bay leaf
1 t salt
½ t white pepper
¼ cup sherry
   Sour cream

In large kettle add water to ham hocks and simmer until meat is tender. Remove meat and cut into small pieces. Set aside. To ham stock add peas, carrots, onion and spices. Simmer 1½ to 2 hours or until peas are cooked and soup is thick. Add ham and sherry. If soup is too thick, add small amount of water. Heat to boiling. Top servings with 1 T sour cream. Serves 10.

Take three pubic hairs and three from the left armpit. Burn them on a hot shovel. Pulverize and insert into a piece of bread. Dip bread in soup and feed to a lover.

*— Albertus Magnus,
medieval occultist and philosopher*

SOUP a L'OIGNON

4 medium onions, sliced thin
3 T butter
4 cups brown beef stock
½ t Worcestershire sauce
1 t salt
¼ t pepper
1 clove garlic
4 slices French bread
  Parmesan cheese

Saute onions in butter until golden brown. Add stock, Worcestershire, salt and pepper. Simmer slowly until onions are tender. Rub soup tureen with garlic. Toast French bread until very crisp. Place bread and soup in tureen and sprinkle with Parmesan cheese. Serves 4.

VEGETABLES & EXOTIC PLANTS

To modern man it may seem incomprehensible that common vegetables such as beans, peas, carrots, and many others which we take for granted were numbered among the world's aphrodisiacs. But the fact is that the vegetable kingdom claims more lust-provoking foods than any other. Primitive man, on the other hand, took for granted the magical powers of plants and animals. Vegetables were often incorporated into his fertility rites.

Many primitive fertility rites survive today, mainly in marriage rituals. In Europe peas are still thrown into the lap of a bride to bestow fertility, while in the Americas newlyweds are showered with rice. Other vegetables owe their aphrodisiac reputation to their phallic shapes; some were valued merely because they were scarce or expensive. Onions are thought to create sperm. Asparagus and artichokes are reputed to cause urogenital stimulation. Still others are rich in vitamin E, the "anti-sterility" vitamin. If modern man is a bit skeptical as to the erotic value of such common fare as potatoes and beans, there is for him a fascination with the more exotic plants of legend and folklore

One of the oldest and most exotic love plants is Satyrion, whose very name implies its potency. Satyrion was the food of the wine-pouring Satyrs, lecherous demigods of Greek mythology. The Roman historian Theophrastus observed that Satyrion mixed with goat's milk led to no less than seventy consecutive acts of coitus. According to the erotologist John Davenport, modern satyrion *(orchis mascula)*, when applied to the genitals, will enable a man to perform twelve times in a single night. Two other ancient Greek aphrodisiacs were rocket *(brasica eruca)*, and eryngoes *(eryngium maritimum)*. Rocket was used as an offering to be sown around the shrine of the phallic god Priapus. Eryngoes, or sea-holly root, were served candied to stimulate and strengthen the genitalia and survived into Elizabethan times when they were known as "Kissing Comfits."

One of the most exotic love plants of all is the legendary mandrake *(mandragora officinarum)*. It is with this strange plant of the potato family that Leah seduced Jacob in Genesis, and it is also mentioned in the Song of Solomon. The ancient Egyptians called mandrake the "Phallus of the Field." The

Greeks sometimes referred to Aphrodite as "Mandragoritis" (She of the Mandrakes), and they believed that the plant belonged to Circe the witch.

Mandrakes were popular ingredients in witches' brews and love potions in the Middle Ages, but in order to be effective they had to be taken from the spot where a hanged criminal — preferably a rapist — had ejaculated at the moment of death. The method of gathering the mandrakes was also critical. They were pulled screaming from the ground by mangy curs who were then immediately put to death, as they were cursed to go mad. Shakespeare refers to the shrieking mandrakes in *Romeo and Juliet:* "And shrieks like mandrakes torn out of the earth, that living mortals, hearing them, run mad." The aphrodisiac properties of the plant are found in its roots, which are often forked and resemble the trunk and legs of a man. The ancients improved on the image by carving male and female genitalia in the appropriate spot. Today mandrake can be purchased as the drug mandragorine, the sulphate of which is a narcotic similar to atropine.

Another exotic plant which resembles mandrake in appearance and aphrodisiac qualities is ginseng, which the Chinese call *goo-lai-sam.* Like Mandrake the plant is said to be most effective when the root forms the body of a man. It was the Chinese passion for ginseng which first opened China to American trade. The first American ship to reach China arrived at Canton harbor in 1784 with forty tons of domestic ginseng in its hold, destined to be brewed into an aphrodisiac tea. The Chinese believe that their home grown variety must be dug up at midnight, during a full moon, to be a proper love stimulant.

The word "vegetable," from the Latin *vegetus,* means to be active and lively, and vegetarians are said to be spirited lovers. Your garden is a treasury of textures and flavors worthy of the most jaded paramour or gourmet. It is a depository of foods warranted to bewitch, bedazzle and beguile.

VEGETABLES & EXOTIC PLANTS

The decoction of the [asparagus] roots boiled in wine and being taken fasting several mornings together, stirreth up bodily lust in man or woman, whatever some have written to the contrary.

– Nicholas Culpeper,
Culpeper's Complete Herbal, *1652*

TIPS AND WINE

1 lb. cooked asparagus tips
¼ cup Traminer
¼ cup olive oil
¼ t Worcestershire sauce
1/8 dry mustard
   Salt and freshly ground pepper to taste

Arrange asparagus in serving dish. Blend remaining ingredients and mix well. Pour wine dressing over tips and chill several hours. Serves 4.

Dress and cook the asparagus sticks in the normal way by plunging them into boiling water. Slice them obliquely towards the tips into pieces no bigger than the little finger. Take only the choicest sections, and keeping them hot, allow them to drain while the sauce is being prepared in the manner following. —Work ten grammes of flour and a lump of butter together, add salt, a good pinch of powdered nutmeg and the yolks of two eggs diluted with four spoonfuls of water acidulated with lemon juice. After cooking this sauce, drop in the asparagus tips and serve in a covered casserole.

— Madame de Pompadour's Recipe

ASPARAGUS ERECTUS

12 small asparagus tips
4 medium tomatoes
   Salt and pepper to taste
¼ cup melted butter
¼ cup buttered French bread crumbs
¼ cup Romano cheese

Boil asparagus in salted water until nearly tender. Drain. Scald tomatoes; peel and core. Place tomatoes in baking dish. Dip cooked asparagus in melted butter. Stand 3 stalks of asparagus in each tomato. Pour remaining butter over tomatoes. Sprinkle with bread crumbs and cheese. Bake in 350° oven for 25 minutes. Serves 4.

He who boils asparagus, and then fries them in fat, and then pours upon them the yolks of eggs with pounded condiments, and eats every day this dish, will grow very strong for the coitus, and find in it a stimulant for his amorous desires.

— Shaykh Nefzawi,
The Perfumed Garden,
16th century Arabian love manual

ASPARAGUS OMELET

3 eggs
2 T water
¼ t Worcestershire sauce
¼ t paprika
   Salt and lemon pepper to taste
1½ T butter
4 warm asparagus tips

Beat eggs, water, Worcestershire and seasonings. Melt butter in 8 inch skillet. Pour in egg mixture. Tilt skillet so uncooked egg will float to bottom. When omelet is set but still moist, slip to warm platter. Fill with asparagus tips and fold in half. Serves 2.

If your wife is old and your member is exhausted, eat onions in plenty.

*— Martial,
1st century Roman epigrammatist*

ROMAN ORGY ONIONS

4 large onions
1 clove garlic, chopped
1 stalk celery, chopped
6 large fresh mushrooms, chopped
1½ T olive oil
1 t marjoram
½ cup dry bread crumbs
2 T white wine
2 T grated cheese
   Pinch of cayenne
   Salt to taste
   Butter for baking dish

Peel onions and boil in salted water for 15 minutes. Drain and rinse in cold water. Remove centers, leaving a shell 3 layers thick. Chop ½ removed onion pulp and set aside. In small skillet saute garlic, celery and mushrooms in olive oil until cooked. In bowl combine sauteed mixture, onion pulp, marjoram, bread crumbs, wine, cheese, cayenne and salt. Mix thoroughly and stuff shells. Place stuffed onions in buttered baking dish and bake in 350° oven for 25 minutes. Serves 4.

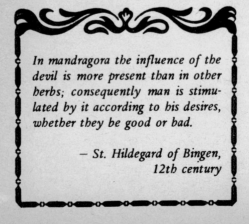

In mandragora the influence of the devil is more present than in other herbs; consequently man is stimulated by it according to his desires, whether they be good or bad.

— St. Hildegard of Bingen, 12th century

Asked about bulbs, I answered: (they can be eaten boiled) in water for those who seek the door of love, or, as they are served with a legitimate wedding meal, but also with pine-kernels or flavoured with rocket and pepper.

— Marcus Terentius Varro,
1st century B.C.

CONNUBIAL ONIONS

18 small white onions
4 T butter
½ t sugar
½ cup Parmesan cheese
¼ cup sherry
   Salt and pepper to taste

Boil onions until tender. Drain. Melt butter in skillet and add remaining ingredients. Stir mixture over low heat about 5 minutes. Place onions in serving dish and cover with sauce. Serves 6.

The next in order you shall have
A large Potato, and a brave:
It must be roased in the fire
That Cupid kindled with desire.
The roasting it will mickle [much] cost;
It will bast itself when it is roast,
It needs no sugar, nor no spice
'T will please a Stomach n'er so nice.

— A New Year Gift, 1661

CUPID'S ROASTED POTATOES

4 baking potatoes
4 slices bacon
  Bacon drippings
4 T light cream
3 T butter
2 T Roquefort cheese
1 T minced parsley
  Salt and pepper to taste

Fry bacon crisp and crumble into bits. Scrub potatoes and rub
skins with bacon drippings. Bake until done. Split in half
lengthwise and rmeove potato from shells. Whip potatoes,
butter, cream, parsley, cheese, salt and pepper until smooth.
Spoon potato mixture into shells. Brown under broiler.
Garnish with bacon bits. Serves 4.

*Will your lordship please to taste a fine potato? 'Twill advance
your withered state, Fill your honor with noble itches.*

— *John Fletcher,*
The Loyal Subject, *1618*

STUD SPUDS

6 medium potatoes, peeled
1 t salt
6 green onions, minced
  Warm milk
  Butter

Quarter potatoes and boil in salted water until tender. Drain
and mash. Gradually add milk and butter to desired
consistency. Whip in onion. Return to low heat until mixture
is hot. Serve with pat of butter. Serves 6.

Let the sky rain potatoes
And again,
How the devil luxury
with his fat rump and potato
finger tickles these together!

– Shakespeare,
The Merry Wives of Windsor, *1602*

SWEET POTATOES SUCCUBUS

6 medium sweet potatoes
¾ cup brown sugar
1/3 cup softened butter
4 egg yolks, beaten
2 egg whites, beaten
½ cup sherry
½ t nutmeg
½ t cinnamon

Boil potatoes until tender; peel and mash. Cream sugar and butter, add egg yolks, potatoes, sherry and spices. Fold in egg whites. Place in well buttered baking dish. Place baking dish in pan of warm water. Bake in 350° oven for 40 minutes. Serves 6.

Will your ladyship have a potato pie? 'Tis a stirring good dish for an old lady after a long lent.

– Beaumont and Fletcher

POTENT POTATO PIE

4 medium potatoes, peeled
1 small onion, sliced in rings
1 2 oz. can anchovy fillets
   Butter
   Freshly ground pepper
½ cup warm milk
½ cup warm light cream

Slice potatoes thin. Butter shallow casserole and layer potatoes, onion and anchovies. Repeat layers. Pour milk and cream over potato mixture. Dot with butter and sprinkle with pepper. Bake in 325° oven for 50 minutes. Serves 4. (Scandinavian anchovies must be used in this recipe.)

In 1132 the monks of Cluny, under the pious leadership of Peter the Venerable, were forbidden to eat pimento because of its lust-provoking qualities.

PROVOCATIVE PIMENTO-RICE

1 large onion, chopped
1 green pepper, chopped
½ cup oil
3 cups rice
2 cups chicken broth
4 cups water
1 4 oz. jar pimentos, drained and chopped
1 3½ oz. jar capers, drained
   Salt to taste

Saute onion and pepper in oil until soft. Add rice and brown lightly. Stir in broth, water, pimentos, capers and salt. Cover tightly and cook over low heat for 35 minutes. Do not remove cover while rice is cooking. Serves 10.

Take seeds of the White Tal-makhana and the Devabhat [wild rice], of each ten Mashas, mix with equal weight of honey, and eat at night. The effect will be enormous vigour and the enjoyment of a hundred women.

– *Kalyana Malla,*
The Ananga Ranga,
16th century Hindu love manual

You must know that nothing is so sure to make women conceive, as a draught composed of Mandrago-la. This is a fact which I have verified upon four occasions, and had it not been for the virtues of this plant, the Queen of France, as well as many noble ladies of that kingdom, would have proven barren.

– *Macchiavelli,*
La Mandragora

WILD OVEN RICE

1 cup wild rice
1¾ cups consomme
1 cup sliced mushrooms
3 T butter

Wash rice several times in cold water. Butter casserole and add rice and consomme. Let stand 3 hours. Cover casserole and bake in 350° oven for 45 minutes, adding a little water if rice becomes too dry. Saute mushrooms in butter until tender and stir into rice mixture. Uncover casserole and bake in 300° oven until all liquid is absorbed. Serves 4.

Green peas, boiled carefully with onions, and powdered with cinnamon, ginger and cardamoms, well pounded, create for the consumer amorous passion and strength in coitus.

— Shaykh Nefzawi,
The Perfumed Garden,
16th century Arabian love manual

PETIT POIS

2 Italian sausages
2 T olive oil
1 onion, chopped
½ lb. mushrooms, sliced
1 package frozen petit pois, thawed
1 cup white rice
2 cups chicken broth
2 T butter
  Salt to taste
  Parmesan cheese

Boil sausages for 10 minutes. Cool and slice. In large kettle heat olive oil and saute sausages, onion and mushrooms until lightly browned. Add peas, rice, broth, butter and salt. Cover tightly and steam for 20 minutes. Before serving, sprinkle with cheese. Serves 4.

In the Arabia of Alladin and Scheherazade, the long, slender carrot was highly esteemed as a potent aphrodisiac. The Arabs spiced their carrots and cooked them in milk in the belief that the erotic effects would be doubled.

CARROT SOUFFLÉ ARABIQUE

2 cups cooked carrots, mashed
1 cup thick white sauce, cooled
3 eggs, separated
½ t nutmeg
1 T chopped parsley
  Salt to taste

Beat egg yolks. Add white sauce, carrots, nutmeg, parsley and salt. Beat egg whites and fold into cooled carrot mixture. Pour into buttered ring mold. Place mold in pan of warm water. Bake in 350° oven for 45 minutes. Serves 6.

Artichokes! Artichokes!
Heats the body and the spirit.
Heats the genitals.

—Parisian street vendor's cry

HOT ARTICHOKE BAKE

1½ T butter
2 T flour
  Salt to taste
  Pinch of cayenne
1½ cups milk
1 t Worcestershire sauce
¼ cup sherry
½ lb. mushrooms, sliced
1 8½ oz. can artichoke hearts, halved
¾ lb. fresh crab meat
  Parmesan cheese

Melt butter and blend in flour, salt and cayenne. Add milk, Worcestershire and sherry and stir until sauce thickens. Saute mushrooms with additional butter. Butter casserole and line with artichoke hearts. Top with crab, mushrooms and sauce. Sprinkle with cheese. Bake in 350° oven for 35 minutes. Serves 4.

A dish of eggplant, cooked in a flour paste and seasoned with pimentos, chives, pepper-corns and vanilla, is considered an aphrodisiac in the West Indies.

EGGPLANT EROTIQUE

1 large eggplant
½ cup flour
¼ cup olive oil
1 clove garlic, chopped
1 onion, chopped
1 8 oz. can tomato sauce
2/3 cup water
1 t choppd chives
2 t chopped pimento
½ t oregano
½ t basil
    Salt and pepper to taste
¾ cup Parmesan cheese
1¼ cup Mozzarella cheese

Peel eggplant and slice ¼ inch thick. Dust eggplant with flour and brown lightly in olive oil. Saute garlic and onion until soft. In small bowl combine onion, garlic, tomato sauce, water and spices. Arrange eggplant, tomato mixture and cheeses in alternate layers in greased casserole. Bake in 350° oven for 35 minutes. (Eggplant should be soaked in cold salted water for 1 hour before slicing.) Serves 6.

They [chick peas] are under the dominion of Venus. They are thought to increase sperm.

— Nicholas Culpeper,
Culpeper's Complete Herbal, *1652*

MISSOV SISSAIR

1 lb. boned lamb, cubed
2 small onions, chopped
1 clove garlic, minced
3 T olive oil
1 cup water
½ t cumin
½ t basil
1 t paprika
   Salt and pepper to taste
1 cup fresh tomatoes, peeled and chopped
¾ cup cooked chick peas

Saute meat, onions and garlic in olive oil until lightly browned. Add water and spices. Simmer for 45 minutes, adding more water if necessary. Add tomatoes and chick peas. Simmer for 30 minutes longer. Serve over hot rice. Serves 4.

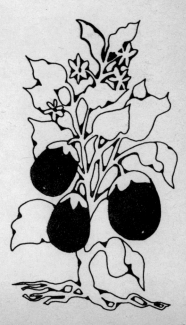

My love hung limp beneath the leaf,
   (O bitter, bitter shame!)
My heavy heart was full of grief
   Until my lady came.

She brought a tasty dish to me,
   (O swollen pod and springing seed!)
My love sprang out right eagerly
   To serve me in my need.

– *Old English Ballad,*
The Love Bean

CREAMY LOVE BEANS

1½ lbs. green beans
½ cup sour cream
½ cup mayonnaise
1½ t capers
2 T chopped pimento
1 green onion, minced

Clean beans and cook in salted water until tender. In saucepan combine remaining ingredients and heat slowly. Pour cream sauce over drained green beans. Serves 6.

The beards of barbel serv'd instead of salads;
Oil'd mushrooms; and the swelling unctuous paps
Of a fat pregnant sow, newly cut off,
Drest with an exquisite and poignant sauce.

– *Ben Johnson,*
The Alchemist, *1610*

EXOTIC STUFFED MUSHROOMS

12 large mushrooms
4 T butter
1½ t minced green onions
1 t minced parsley
6 T finely chopped cooked ham
1½ T mayonnaise
1½ t sherry
¼ t dry mustard
   Salt and pepper to taste
   Parmesan cheese

Wash mushrooms and remove stems. Chop stems fine and saute in 2 T butter (about 5 minutes). Brush mushroom heads with remaining butter. In bowl combine stems, onion, parsley, ham, mayonnaise, sherry, mustard, salt and pepper. Stuff mushroom heads with filling and sprinkle with cheese. Bake in 350° oven for 20 minutes. Yields 12 Hors d'Oeuvres.

The flowers and leaves of myrtle, two handfuls, infuse them in two quarts spring water, and a quart of white wine, for twenty four hours, and then distill them in a cold still and this will be a strong scent and tincture, and by adding more or less of the myrtle you may make it stronger or weaker as you please. This beautifies and mixed with cordial syrups is a good cordial and inclines those that drink it to be very amorous.

— Middle Ages Love tonic

If envious age relax the nuptial knot,
Thy food be mushrooms, and thy feast shallot.

— Martial,
1st century Roman epigrammatist

NUPTIAL KNOT SHALLOTS

1 lb. mushrooms, sliced
3 shallots, minced
1 T fresh chopped parsley
¼ cup sherry
6 T butter
　　Salt and pepper to taste

Saute mushrooms, shallots and parsley in butter until soft. Add wine, salt and pepper. Simmer over low heat for 5 minutes. Serve over meat or hot toast. Serves 4.

The sap of mallows, as well as three of its roots bound together, excited the passion of women.

— Pliny the Elder,
Roman encyclopedist, 1st century A.D.

MAD MALCOLM'S MALLOWS

2 lbs. young mallow leaves
2 T butter
2 T flour
　　Pinch of cayenne
　　Salt to taste
1¼ cups milk
½ cup mild yellow cheese, grated
2 hard cooked eggs, sliced

Wash leaves and cook in salted water until leaves are tender. Drain and keep warm. Melt butter and blend in flour, salt and cayenne. Add milk and cheese; stir until cheese melts and sauce thickens. Pour sauce over greens and garnish with sliced egg. Serves 6.

Tomatoes are believed to have originated in Peru. They were introduced to Europe by the Spaniards in the 16th century. Because tomatoes were thought to stimulate sexuality, they were called "love apples" in Europe.

STUFFED LOVE APPLES

4 large tomatoes
1 lb. fresh cooked shrimp
2 T olive oil
2 T wine vinegar
1 t prepared mustard
3 green onions, minced
2 T minced celery
    Salt and freshly ground pepper to taste

Wash tomatoes and core. Slice tomatoes into fourths, halfway down. Sprinkle with salt and pepper. Chill. In bowl blend oil, vinegar, mustard, onion and celery. Add shrimp and marinate for 2 hours. Stuff tomatoes with shrimp and sprinkle with marinade. Serves 4.

Men become passionately attached to women who know how to cosset them with delicate titbits.

– Honore de Balzac

STACKED TOMATOES

2 large ripe tomatoes
½ cup cooked diced chicken
¼ cup diced celery
¼ cup cooked diced chestnuts
1 T chopped pimento
1 hard cooked egg, chopped
1/3 cup mayonnaise
  Salt and pepper to taste
2 sprigs parsley
  Crisped salad greens

Cut each tomato into three slices. Combine remaining ingredients except lettuce and parsley. Mix lightly and spread mixture on tomato slices. Layer tomatoes using 3 slices per portion. Garnish with parsley and place on greens. Serves 2.

Scientists at Edinburgh University's endocrinology research unit recently discovered that a man's sex hormones run highest between 4 in the morning and noon. About 8 in the evening they're at the very lowest level, contrary to the time-honored regimen for seduction.

– San Francisco Examiner, -(WNS)

Let's drink the health of truffles black;
In gratitude we must not lack.
For they assure us dominance
In all erotic dalliance.
As an aid to lovers' bliss
Fate pleasurably fashioned this
Rarity, divine godsend,
To use forever without end.

— French poem eulogizing truffles

TRUFFLE SAUCE

1 T butter
1/3 cup dry white wine
3 T brandy
3 medium-sized truffles, peeled and chopped
6 green shallot tops, chopped fine

Melt butter and add remaining ingredients. Cook over medium heat 6 minutes or until the liquid is almost evaporated. Serve over fillet of beef. Serves 2.

The truffle, praised by Brillat-Savarin as "the diamond of the kitchen," is a fungus which grows on the subterranean roots of trees. It is located and rooted up by specially trained dogs and pigs. The delicate truffle has been eulogized as an appetizer for venereal desire by such notable epicures as Louis XIV, Madame du Barry and the infamous Marquis de Sade.

TRUFFLED VEAL

1½ lbs. veal medallions
3 T butter
5 T finely minced ham
1½ T chopped parsley
2 shallots, minced
1 truffle, chopped
½ cup Marsala
   Salt and pepper to taste

Pound veal medallions until very flat. Melt butter in skillet; add veal and brown quickly on both sides. Add remaining ingredients and simmer covered for about 7 minutes or until meat is tender. Serves 4.

A special "Venus hamper" of supposed aphrodisiac products is being offered to Christmas shoppers by Fauchon's, a fashionable Paris grocery store.

It contains such delicacies as birds nest soup, quails' eggs, stuffed pimentoes and candied ginger, and costs $33.

— Reuters News Service, 1969

St. Jerome divided his buns among the hungry, but not his beans. He forbid his nuns to eat beans because in partibus genitalibus titillationes producunt *(beans excite genital titillation)*.

SAUCY BEAN SALAD

1 lb. small white beans
1 small onion, sliced
6 cloves
½ t oregano

Soak beans overnight in cold water. Drain. Cover beans with fresh water and cook with onion, cloves and oregano until beans are tender. Add salt about 30 minutes before beans are cooked. Drain and remove cloves; set aside to cool.

For Sauce:

¼ cup olive oil
2 cloves garlic, chopped
2 cups tomato sauce
¼ cup water
½ t oregano
¼ t basil
   Salt and pepper to taste

Saute garlic in oil until soft. Add remaining ingredients and simmer for 30 minutes or until sauce is slightly thickened. Set aside to cool.

For Filling & Topping:

3 2 oz. cans sardines, packed in oil
1 hard cooked egg, grated
2 T chopped parsley

In salad bowl arrange in alternate layers beans, sardines and tomato sauce. Top with grated egg and chopped parsley. Chill. Serves 10.

Spinach has been reputed for ages to maintain strength and restore virility. Spinach is a powerful source of vitamins and minerals, especially iron, which is essential for sexual vigor. According to legend, spinach was the favorite food of the Blessed Virgin Mary.

BAKED SPINACH

2 packages frozen chopped spinach, thawed
1 pt. sour cream
2 cans cream of potato soup, undiluted
   Salt and pepper to taste
   Parmesan cheese

Completely drain all water from spinach. Add sour cream, potato soup, salt and pepper. Place in large buttered baking dish. Sprinkle with Parmesan cheese. Bake in 350° oven for 50 minutes. Serves 6.

Radishes frequently appeared on the lavish banquet tables of 16th century Europe. These hot little vegetables were so highly esteemed as love stimulants that a poem entitled Raporum Encompium *(Eulogy of Radishes) was published in 1540 at Lyons by Claude Bigothier.*

RAVISHING RADISH DIP

3 bunches radishes, cleaned
1 cup sour cream
3 oz bleu cheese
3 t chives
½ t flavored salt
¼ t dill weed

Chill radishes. Combine sour cream and cheese until well blended. Stir in chives, salt and dill weed. Use as a dip with chilled radishes.

MEAT & GAME

Both fact and fancy have contributed to the age old reputation of certain meats and game as aphrodisiacs. Primitives consume the flesh of animals to absorb not only the physical characteristics of the animal, but its moral and intellectual attributes. If the animal is considered divine, then its divinity, too, is passed on to the consumer. Lion heart brings strength to the African Suk; some American Indians ate deer meat to be fleet of foot, and bear meat bestowed courage. The sexual organs of animals were believed to stimulate desire for obvious reasons.

The hearty Tartars put their faith in penis of horse, the American Indians in beaver testicles, and the Australian aborigine in kangaroo testicles. Mountain oysters (bull and sheep testicles) are still eaten today the world over. In the American Ozarks these tasty delicacies are tossed into a fire and roasted until they pop. Rabbit is a traditional fertility symbol, leading men to believe that if they ate of the rabbit's flesh they would be able to perform as well — and as often. The ancients believed that the liver was the seat of sexual desire; by association the liver of animals was highly prized as an aphrodisiac.

Not only the flesh, but other parts of animals were believed to excite passion. Contemporary shops in Hong Kong yield such exotic love stimulants as powdered deer antlers *(lu kung)* and rhinocerous horn *(hsi chio)*. The tooth, nail, horn and hair of rhinocerous has become so sought after in modern times that at least three species of Asian rhino are in imminent danger of extinction. Bull's urine, crocodile semen and sparrow's brains were ancient favorites. Marinated sow's vulva is highly recommended by the 3rd century Roman cook, Apicius.

The most famous animal in aphrodisiac lore is the skink, called *scinus* by the Romans. The skink is a long, crocodile-like lizard native to North Africa. Its feet, snout and genitals were pounded together with various herbs and served in wine. According to Pliny, the skink was an invigorating aphrodisiac and an antidote to poison. The Persians also hunted the skink *(seck-amkaer)* to prepare a powerful love potion by mixing its flesh with amber, ground pearls, saffron and opium.

Meats are analeptic, that is, giving or restoring strength.

According to Brillat-Savarin, the active ingredient in animal fibre is azezome, a substance which gives the brown and red color to cooked and uncooked meat. Dark fleshed meat is particularly abundant in azezome, as is beef, mutton, hare and most wild fowl. Meats are also rich in protein, a strength-giving organic substance.

In word origin, the hunt is intimately related to sex. The word "venery," from the French *venerie,* refers to the art or practice of hunting. The same word, "venery," means sexual intercourse or coition. It all depends on what you do with what you catch.

MEAT & GAME

. . . the condition of the body, and consequently the quality of the sperm depends directly upon the food you take. If, therefore, a man will passionately give himself up to the enjoyment of coition, without undergoing too great fatigue, he must live upon strengthening food, exciting comfits, aromatic plants, meat, honey, eggs, and other similar viands.

—Shaykh Nefzawi,
The Perfumed Garden,
16th century Arabian love manual

ESCARGOTS DE JOIE

4 dz. snails, with shells
1 cup softened butter
3 cloves garlic, minced
2 shallots, minced
¼ cup finely chopped parsley
1 T finely chopped black olives
2 T dry white wine
½ t salt
¼ t freshly ground pepper
¼ t nutmeg
  Pinch of cayenne

Set snails and shells aside. Combine remaining ingredients, working mixture into a smooth paste. Place a small lump of butter mixture in shell and add snail. Fill shell with paste until shell is sealed. Place on flat baking tin or escargot pan. Bake in 400° oven for 6 to 8 minutes. Serves 6.

To encourage my jaded body ... I applied myself to strong meats, such as strong broths and eggs, using wine moderately ... so great was my care to acquit myself honourably with my mistress.

— Petronius,
The Satyricon, *1st century A.D.*

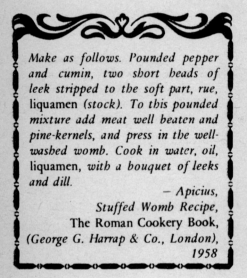

Make as follows. Pounded pepper and cumin, two short heads of leek stripped to the soft part, rue, liquamen (stock). To this pounded mixture add meat well beaten and pine-kernels, and press in the well-washed womb. Cook in water, oil, liquamen, with a bouquet of leeks and dill.

— Apicius,
Stuffed Womb Recipe,
The Roman Cookery Book,
(George G. Harrap & Co., London),
1958

BEEF BRISKET WITH JADED SAUCE

1 3 lb. beef brisket
1 onion, cut in chunks
2 stalks celery, cut in chunks
1 bay leaf
6 peppercorns

Place all ingredients in kettle; cover with water and bring to a boil. Simmer until tender (2 to 2½ hours). Skim as necessary. Serve with Jaded Sauce. Serves 6.

JADED SAUCE

½ cup chopped parsley
½ cup olive oil
1 clove garlic, crushed
¼ cup wine vinegar

Mix all ingredients and serve with sliced Beef Brisket.

Eryngoes are not good for to be taken,
And Lust provoking meats must be forsaken.

     — The Ladies Dictionary, *1649*

LUSTY BARBECUED LIVER

1 lb. beef liver
1 large onion, sliced in rings
2 T butter
1 T vinegar
1 T Worcestershire sauce
1 t brown sugar
1 t prepared mustard
¼ t chili powder
¼ cup catsup
1 T water
 Salt and pepper to taste

Cut liver in 1 inch strips and place in baking pan. Saute onions in butter until lightly browned. Place onions on liver. Mix remaining ingredients and spoon over liver and onions. Bake covered in 325° oven for 25 minutes. Uncover and bake for 10 minutes longer. Serves 4.

[Beefsteak is] probably as powerful a sexual stimulant as any food.

     — Havelock Ellis

BURGUNDY BEEF

2 lbs. beef steak
2 T flour
10 small white onions, sliced
2 T bacon drippings
½ cup beef bouillon
1 cup Burgundy
¼ t thyme
¼ t marjoram
1 bay leaf
   Salt and pepper to taste
½ lb. mushrooms, sliced

Cut beef in strips and dust with flour. Saute beef and onions in bacon drippings until browned. Add bouillon, Burgundy and spices. Simmer over low heat for 1½ hours. Add mushrooms; simmer 30 minutes longer. Add more bouillon or wine if necessary. Serves 4.

This acid milk [yogurt] awakens the desire for coitus in warm natures and makes the mucous membrane moist.

– Avicenna,
Islamic philosopher and physician

VEAL LOAF

1½ lbs. ground veal
2 cups grated raw carrots
1 onion, finely chopped
1 3 oz. can chopped mushrooms, drained
½ cup dry bread crumbs
1 t salt
¼ t pepper
1 cup yogurt

Mix all ingredients in a bowl. When thoroughly mixed, press into a greased loaf pan. Bake in 375° oven about 1½ hours. Remove from oven and let stand 10 minutes. Pour off any liquid and turn loaf out on hot platter. Serves 6.

. . . we merely state a fact, which is that spicy dishes, truffles, game, and old wines possess, indirectly perhaps but no less undoubtedly, the property of stimulating the sexual appetites.

– Dr. Jacobus X,
The Genital Laws, *1900*

BUCK STEAK

3 lbs. venison steak, 1 inch thick
1 cup milk
½ cup flour
3 T bacon drippings
1 onion, chopped
1 clove garlic, minced
1 T chopped parsley
½ cup chopped celery
½ cup chopped green pepper
1 cup tomato sauce
½ cup dry red wine
¼ cup water
1 bay leaf
½ t allspice
    Salt and pepper to taste

Soak steak in milk 4 to 5 hours. Drain and dry. Dust with flour and fry in bacon drippings until well browned. Place steak in heavy casserole and add remaining ingredients. Cover and bake in 350° oven for 2 hours or until tender, basting often. Add more water is necessary. Serves 6.

Boil 4 bull's testicles together with salt. Cut into slices and sprinkle with salt, pepper, nutmeg and cinnamon. In a pie crust, place layers of sliced testicles alternated with a mince of lamb's kidneys, ham, marjoram, cloves and thyme.

– 16th century
Pie of Bull's Testicles recipe,
Bartolomeo Scappi,
cook to Pope Pius V

MOUNTAIN OYSTERS

20 lamb's testicles
  Juice of 1 lemon
  Butter
2 cloves garlic, minced
2 T chopped parsley
¼ cup dry white wine

Remove membranes from testicles and soak overnight in lemon juice and enough cold water to cover. Drain and dry. Melt butter in skillet, add testicles and cook slowly on both sides until tender. Add garlic, parsley and wine and simmer a few minutes longer. Serves 4.

> *Take one cockroach, one salamander and a piece of cotton that has dried a penis after intercourse. Dry and mix well. Conceal in a loved one's food.*
>
> *— Mossi love recipe*

Take a Rump of Beef, and season it with Nutmegs grated, and some Pepper and Salt mingled together, and season the Beef on the bony side; lay it in a pipkin with the fat side downward. Take three pints of Elder-wine vinegar, and as much water, and three great Onions, and a bunch of Rosemary tied up together: put them all into the pipkin, and stew them three or four hours together with a soft fire, being covered close. Then dish it up upon sippets, blowing off the fat from the Gravy; and some of the Gravy put on to the beef, and serve it up.

*— 17th century Aphrodisiac
Rump of Beef recipe*

RUMP OF BEEF

4 lbs. pot roast of beef
2 cups vinegar
2 cups water
1 large onion, sliced
¼ cup sugar
2 t salt
10 peppercorns
3 whole cloves
2 bay leaves

Place meat in bowl and set aside. Combine remaining ingredients in saucepan and heat to boiling. Pour hot mixture over meat. Cool. Add 1 slice lemon. Cover and place in refrigerator. Marinate meat 4 days, turning twice daily. Remove meat from marinade and drain. Strain marinade and reserve. Melt 3 T butter in heavy skillet, add meat and brown on all sides. Add 3 cups marinade and bring to boil. Reduce heat, cover, and cook slowly for 2½ to 3 hours. Add more marinade if necessary. Remove meat to platter and keep warm. Reserve liquid for gravy.

For Gravy:

¼ cup butter
¼ cup flour
2 cups marinade
½ cup sour cream

In pan melt butter and blend in flour. Slowly add marinade and stir constantly until mixture thickens. Add sour cream and cook until heated. Do not boil. Serve with potato pancakes. Serves 8.

Sea and sky have not been left untapped by man in his quest for aphrodisiac substances. The sea, with its myriad life forms, has yielded a vast variety of foods to nourish the passions and kindle the genital fires. Art and mythology have also contributed heavily to the marriage of seafood and love food.

Aphrodite herself was born of the sea. After Kronos killed and castrated his father he threw his genitals into the sea. About them a foam gathered from which sprang Aphrodite. (The Greek word *aphros* means foam.) There are actually three Aphrodites: Aphrodite Urania, goddess of ideal love; Aphrodite Genetrix, who received prayers from women seeking husbands; and Aphrodite Prone, patroness of prostitutes and goddess of physical love. The 15th century Italian painter, Botticelli, represented Venus' birth in a famous painting entitled "The Birth of Venus." Sometimes loosely referred to as "Venus on the Half-Shell," the masterpiece pictures the nude goddess standing in a huge seashell modestly hiding her *mons veneris* with her long flowing hair. This painting is one of many which characterized the goddess as a sea deity, and suggested the erotic properties of seafood.

The mere mention of the word "aphrodisiac" conjures up visions of oysters in most minds. The oyster's reputation is due to its mucuous consistency and its resemblance to the female genitalia. Oysters should be eaten raw for maximum potency. If you are planning to dine with a prostitute, the Greek poet Asclepiades recommends a meal of three large and ten small fish, and twenty-four prawns. Ancient Romans believed shellfish were especially invigorating, and they frequently added zest to their libidinous appetites with a diet of eel, octopus and squid, all having obvious phallic associations.

Fish are extremely fertile, laying profuse numbers of eggs. Fish roe, especially that of cod and herring, ranks high on the list of aphrodisiac foods. But it is the grey transparent sturgeon eggs used for fine Russian caviar which are the most captivating. Chinese *bon vivants* are fond of seahorses and shark's fin. The Japanese, whose geography makes them extremely dependent on the sea for food, are the most skilled in the preparation of seafood for epicurean delights and carnal pleasures. In modern Japan divers risk life and limb daily to hunt ferocious sharks for their prized fins, which bring high prices in the shops of Hong Kong. Fish is rich in iodine and phosphorous, substances favoring the reproductive system.

Aphrodite Prone is frequently depicted with a phallic goose, symbol of Priapus, whose neck and head typify the *membrum virile.* Aphrodite Urania is often pictured riding on a swan. It is the genitals of fowl which are most sought after for their provocative influence. Swan's pizzles and hummingbird hearts will make one wanton, but in the absence of such esoteric items, pheasant, turkey or goose will do nicely.

Bishop Burchard of Worms, in his book of penances, De Poenitentia Decretorum, *describes a medieval practice in which women placed a small live fish in their center of being. When the fish expired it was fried and given to a lover as an aphrodisiac.*

Among the Ponapeans a similar custom is practiced whereby a small fish is gently sucked and licked from the woman's vulva as foreplay to sexual intercourse.

SPICY TROUT TREAT

4 brook trout, cleaned
   Salt
½ cup dry bread crumbs
2 t minced parsley
¼ t nutmeg
¼ t thyme
   Pinch of saffron
   Freshly ground pepper
½ cup dry white wine

Sprinkle fish with salt. In bowl combine crumbs, parsley and spices. Generously butter large baking dish and cover bottom with half of crumb mixture. Place fish on crumbs and add wine. Sprinkle remaining crumbs on fish and bake in 350° oven for 25 minutes, basting frequently. Serves 2.

Old impotent Alden from Walden
Ate salmon to heat him to scaldin'.
  'Twas just the ticket,
  To stiffen his wicket,
This salmon of Amorous Alden.

– Anon

SALMON OF AMOROUS ALDEN

3 lbs. salmon fillets, with skin
¼ cup wine vinegar
¼ cup tomato catsup
½ t celery seed
1/8 t rosemary
½ t oregano
1/8 t dry mustard
¼ t sugar
¼ t salt
  Freshly ground pepper

Place fillets in container for marinating. Combine remaining ingredients and pour over salmon. Marinate for 3 hours. Barbecue over hot coals until done, turning only once. Baste frequently with marinade. Remove skins and serve. Serves 6.

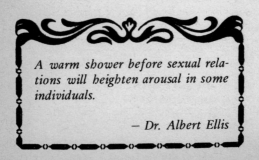

A warm shower before sexual relations will heighten arousal in some individuals.

– Dr. Albert Ellis

Take yor eeles and rub them with salt till all the skinne bee quite taken off. Then slitt them downe the belly. Then wash them very cleane. Then take some sweet marjorum & shredd them with cloves, mace, nutmeg, pepper and salt. Season it & tye it up very close with paper. Then take a pinte of white wine & a quart of water & lett it boyle. Then putt yor eele & lett it boyle till it bee tender and putt to it while it boyles a bunch of sweet hearbs and some whole spice. Then take your liquor and lett it cooke and when cold, putt in yor eele & soe lett stand for yor use.

– *Ye Collar Eele recipe,*
Lucayos Cook Book, *1660*

EEL STEW

2 lbs. eel, cleaned and skinned
2 T olive oil
1 onion, chopped
1 clove garlic, chopped
2 T flour
1 cup water
½ cup dry red wine
½ t oregano
1 bay leaf
1½ t parsley
   Salt and pepper to taste

Heat oil and saute onion and garlic. Stir in flour gradually. Add water, wine, spices and parsley. Cut eel in 1 inch slices and add to sauce. Simmer for 1 hour. Serves 6.

Who lewdly dancing at a midnight ball
For hot eryngoes and fat oysters call.

– *Juvenal,*
Roman poet, *2nd century A.D.*

STEAK 'N OYSTER PIE

1 lb. round steak
12 oysters
¼ cup butter
    Flour
¾ cup beef bouillon
½ cup hot water
    Pastry for 1 9-inch crust
    Milk

Trim all fat from steak and cut into 24 thin strips. Cut oysters in half. Roll oyster half and small lump of butter in each beef strip. Dredge each roll in flour. Pack rolls in pie tin and pour bouillon and water over top. Cover with pastry. Slit pastry several times to allow steam to escape. Crimp pastry edge and brush with milk. Bake in 350° oven for 1 hour and 15 minutes. Serves 6.

While Venus fills the heart (without heart really
Love, though good always, is not quite so good),
Ceres presents a plate of vermicelli, –
For love must be sustain'd like flesh and blood, –
While Bacchus pours out wine, or hands a jelly:
Eggs, oysters, too, are amatory food;
But who is their purveyor from above
Heaven knows, – it may be Neptune, Pan, or Jove.

– *Lord Byron,*
Don Juan, *1823*

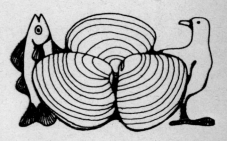

VERMICELLI DON JUAN

1 6½ oz. can minced clams, drained
2 cloves garlic, chopped
3 T olive oil
2 cups tomato sauce
1 cup water
2 t chopped parsley
  Salt and pepper to taste
  Vermicelli

Saute garlic in olive oil until soft and light brown. Discard garlic. To olive oil add clams, tomato sauce, water, parsley, salt and pepper. Simmer slowly, about 45 minutes, or until sauce is thickened. Cook vermicelli. Drain well and cover with clam sauce. If stronger clam taste is desired, add clam juice and cut down proportionately on water. Do not use cheese with this sauce. Serves 4.

In Venice why so many whores abound?
The reason sure is easy to be found,
Because, as learned sages all agree,
Fair Venus' birthplace was the salt, salt sea.

– Anon

HARLOT'S CAVIAR

½ cup caviar
1 T anchovy paste
1 T pimento, mashed
¼ t lemon juice
   Thin cucumber slices
   Toast rounds
   Grated hard-cooked egg

Blend caviar, anchovy paste, pimento, chives and lemon juice. Spread on cucumber slices and place on toast rounds. Garnish with grated egg. Serve as Hors d'Oeuvres.

Oysters, fish, honey, asparagus and spices have been said for centuries to be aphrodisiacs. A low protein diet will inhibit sexuality and one experiment at the University of Minnesota proved that a semi-starvation diet will eventually lead to sexual indifference.

– Dr. Albert Ellis

SEA DREAM SALAD

1 lb. crab meat
¼ cup chopped onion
¼ cup chopped green pepper
¼ cup chopped celery
2 T butter
1 T chopped parsley
½ cup mayonnaise
2 T cream
1 t Worcestershire sauce
½ t dry mustard
  Pepper to taste
½ cup chopped toasted almonds
  Crisp lettuce cups
  Paprika
  Mayonnaise for topping

Saute onion, green pepper and celery in butter until slightly soft. Combine all ingredients except lettuce and paprika. Place in buttered casserole and sprinkle with paprika. Bake in 350° oven for 20 minutes. Serve in lettuce cups and top with mayonnaise. Serves 4.

For what cares the drunken dame?
Take head or tail, to her 'tis much the same
Who at deep midnight on fat oysters sups.

— Juvenal,
Satires, 2nd century A.D.

OYSTER SUPS

1 dz. small oysters
6 slices bacon, halved
   Sliced water chestnuts

Wrap halved bacon slice around each oyster and 1 slice water
chestnut. Fasten with toothpick. Place on rack in baking dish.
Bake in 425° oven until bacon is crisp. Serve as Hors d'Oeuves.

Fish and crustacians have been valued as powerful aphrodisiacs
since antiquity, mainly because they contain large amounts of
phosphorous and iodine. One often repeated folk tale relates
that a drake, after drinking water from a copper vessel
containing phosphorous, immediately set about copulating
himself to death.

CURRIED HALIBUT STEAKS

4 halibut steaks
1 T curry powder
2 T oil
2 T butter
   Sour cream
   Chopped peanuts

Mix curry powder and ginger. Sprinkle on halibut. Heat oil and
butter in large skillet. Pan fry steaks until done. Garnish with
sour cream and peanuts. Serves 4.

Joshua was the son of Nun. Nun in Hebrew is the same word for fish. It also signifies a woman, or, more specifically, the sexual part of a woman.

HEARTS OF PALM NEPTUNE

2 lbs. raw shrimp, peeled and cleaned
   Lemon juice
1 onion, chopped
1 clove garlic, minced
3 T butter
2 large tomatoes, peeled and chopped
1 bay leaf
1 cup hearts of palm, sliced
   Salt and pepper to taste

Marinate shrimp in lemon juice for 1 hour. Drain. Lightly brown onion and garlic in butter. Add tomatoes, shrimp, bay leaf, salt and pepper. Simmer slowly about 15 minutes or until shrimp is cooked. Add hearts of palm and heat through. Remove bay leaf and serve over hot rice. Serves 6.

In marvelous fashion oysters are a stimulant, hence shameless and lascivious women ate oysters in order to be more apt for the amatory act.

– Anon

BEARDED OYSTER BAKE

3 T melted butter
½ t Worcestershire sauce
2 t chopped chives
2 dz. medium oysters

In shallow baking dish pour butter, Worcestershire and chives. Add oysters and bake in 400° oven for 8 minutes or until edges curl. Baste several times with sauce. Serves 4.

KING CRAB LOUIS

1 cup mayonnaise
½ cup chili sauce
1 t horseradish
½ t chopped chives
1 t lemon juice
½ t capers
¼ cup heavy cream, whipped
1 lb. king crab meat
2 hard cooked eggs, sliced
2 tomatoes, cut in wedges
1 cup julienne beets
  Crisped salad greens

Combine first six ingredients and fold in whipped cream.
Arrange crab in center of greens and garnish with eggs,
tomatoes and beets. Top with dressing. Serves 4.

Fish really have the property of bringing the spermatic secretion into activity. They are rich in phosphorus and are usually eaten with a large amount of salt, which adds to their action. Nor would it be possible to deny the value of shell-fish, or of oysters, which Juvenal commends so highly.

– Dr. Jacobus X,
The Genital Laws, *1900*

CREAMY PRAWN SALAD

1 lb. prawns, cooked and shelled
Lemon juice
½ cup sour cream
½ cup mayonnaise
½ cup grated cucumber
2 t capers
¼ t celery salt
   Pinch of cayenne
   Crisped butter lettuce

Sprinkle prawns with lemon juice. Chill. Whip remaining ingredients. Chill. Serve over prawns and crisped lettuce. Serves 6.

Place a live frog in an anthill and leave until the ants have cleaned the bones; then take the heart-shaped bone and the hook-shaped bone; keep the first yourself but hook the second in the clothing of a loved one.

– American Negro folklore

FROG'S LEGS

6 pairs frog's legs
2 cups cold water
2 T vinegar
3½ T butter
2 small cloves garlic, mashed
2 T minced parsley
1 lemon

Soak legs in cold water and vinegar for 2 hours. Saute legs in 2 T butter until golden brown on both sides. Spread legs on serving platter and keep warm. Add additional butter to pan and saute garlic and parsley until butter is lightly browned. Pour butter sauce over legs and sprinkle with lemon. Serves 2.

> *After a perfect meal we are more susceptible to the ecstasy of love than at any other time . . .*
>
> *— Dr. Hans Balzli*

The flesh of the partridge, which is of good and easy digestion, is highly nutritious; it strengthens the brain, facilitates conception, and arouses the half-extinct desire for venereal pleasures.

— Platina,
De Valetudine Tuenda

ROASTED PARTRIDGES

2 partridges, trussed
    Salt and freshly ground pepper to taste
4 slices bacon
2 T melted butter
¼ cup chicken stock
¼ cup white wine

Rub birds with salt and pepper and place on rack in roaster. Cover with sliced bacon. Combine butter, stock and wine; pour over birds. Bake in 325° oven for 45 minutes, basting frequently. Serves 4.

He took two ounces of Chinese cubebs, one ounce of fat extract of Ionian hemp, one ounce of fresh caryophyle, one ounce of red cinnamon from Serendib, ten drachms of white Malabar cardamon, five of Indian ginger, five of white pepper, five of pimento from the isles, one ounce of the berries of Indian star-anise, and half an ounce of mountain thyme. These be mixed cunningly, after having pounded and sieved them. He added pure honey until the whole became a thick paste; then he mingled five grains of musk and an ounce of pounded fish roe with the rest. Finally he added a little concentrated rose-water and put all in the bowl ... saying: "Here is a sovereign mixture which will harden the eggs and thicken the sap when it becomes too thin ... You must eat this paste two hours before the sexual approach, but for three days before that you must eat nothing save roast pigeons excessively seasoned with spice, male fish with the cream complete, and lightly fried ram's eggs. If after all that you do not pierce the very walls of the room and get the foundations of the house with child, you can cut off my beard and spit in my face ..."

— *Tale of Beauty-Spot,*
Arabian Nights

STUFFED QUAIL WITH BAR-LE-DUC SAUCE

12 quail, cleaned
2 cups flour
2 t salt
½ t pepper
½ cup shortening
1 onion, chopped
¾ cup chopped celery
½ cup butter
1 small loaf stale bread
½ t poultry seasoning
1½ T chopped parsley
½ cup chicken broth

Roll quail in flour, salt and pepper. In large skillet heat shortening and brown quail. Saute onion and celery in butter until soft. Crumble bread and combine with onion mixture and remaining ingredients. Stuff birds and place on rack on roaster. Bake in 325° oven for 1½ hours. Serve with Bar-Le-Duc Sauce. Serves 12.

Cook the ground powder of the chrysanthemum stone with water until a thick paste appears. While cooking, stir in the pulverized wings of butterflies. Dry mixture. Add a few drops of honey and roll mixture into tiny pills. A pill must be secreted into the sleeve of the beloved, who is then rendered submissive to all advances.

— Ancient Chinese philtre

BAR-LE-DUC GAME SAUCE

½ cup currant jam
½ cup water
1 T butter
2 T lemon juice
  Pinch of cayenne
3 cloves
1 t salt
½ cup ruby port

Simmer jam, water, butter, lemon juice and seasonings until jam is thoroughly dissolved. Add wine and simmer until heated. Before serving remove cloves. Serve with game. Yields 1½ cups.

HERBS & SPICES

Man's search for the Fountain of Youth, the Elixer of Life — and spices — has changed the map of the world. When Columbus set sail in 1492 he was looking for new trade routes to bring rare and exotic Eastern spices to the tables of Europe. Spices were among the most prized booty of the Crusades, and aromatic seasonings motivated Marco Polo to undertake his epic Eastern journeys. Before the discovery of artificial preservatives and refrigeration, spices were used to add extra piquancy to foods and to disguise the flavor of salted meat and fish. In addition, spices were used extensively as aphrodisiacs.

When eaten in large quantities, as they are in the Near East, spices irritate the bladder and lower urogenital tract, causing direct stimulation. A prime example is Indian curry, which has been used for ages as an aid to love-making. Curry powder is not a spice, but a combination of spices including cumin, coriander seeds, cardamon seeds, ginger, garlic, tumeric, mustard seeds and vinegar.

Herbs have traditionally been associated with love magic and the occult. These magical plants were often included in philtres or worn as amulets to ward off the evil eye. Herbs and spices have been used to deck the bridal bed, and were sown in sacred places as offering to fertility gods. As to the efficacy of herbs and spices as love foods, you must keep in mind the debt that modern medicine owes to herbal lore for many of its miracle drugs.

Condiments exert on the generic appetite a positive influence, due to the congestive action which they produce on the pelvic organs. Pepper, mentioned by Dioscorides, cinnamon, vanilla, mace, pimento, and especially the small red pimento, savory, celebrated in the Priapeiae, and rocket, which according to Columella, "excitat ad Venerem tardos cruca maretos," together with nutmeg and mustard: these are the principal.

– Dr. Jacobus X,
The Genital Laws, *1900*

PIMENTO LOVE CUPS

4 pimento cups
4 eggs
4 T light cream
   Salt and pepper to taste
2 T butter
2 T flour
¼ t dry mustard
1 cup milk
3 T Parmesan cheese
4 slices toast
   Chopped chives

Place pimento cups in individual ramekins and drop raw egg in each cup. Season with salt and pepper and add 1 T cream. Bake in 350° oven until eggs are set. Melt butter and blend in flour and mustard. Pour in milk and stir until sauce thickens. Add cheese. Place pimento cups on toast and cover with sauce. Garnish with chives. Serves 4.

Burdock seeds in a mortar pounde them. Add of three-yeris-old goat ye lefte testycle and from ye back heris of a whyte whelpe one pynche of poudre, ye heris to be cutte on ye firste daye of ye newe mone and burne on ye seventh daye. Infuse alle ye items in a bottel halfe fylled with brandye. Leve uncorked twenty-one dayes to receive astral influence. Cook on ye twenty-firste daye until ye thicke consistency is reched. Add four droppes of crocodyle semen and passe throgh fylter. Rubbe mixture on genitalia and await ye result.

— Grimoire *(Black Book)*,
Middle Ages

BURDOCK GRIMOIRE

1 lb. young burdock leaves
    Salt and pepper to taste
1 T olive oil
1 T butter
1 clove garlic, minced
    Parmesan cheese

Wash leaves and remove burrs. Boil in salted water until tender. Saute garlic in butter and oil; do not brown. Drain leaves and add garlic mixture. Season with salt and pepper. Sprinkle with cheese. Serves 4.

Hot lavender, mints, savory, marjoram . . . are given to men of middle age.

– *Shakespeare,*
The Winter's Tale, *1610*

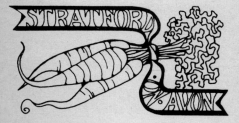

SHAKESPEARE'S CARROT

2 large bunches carrots
3 T butter
3 T catsup
1 T honey
2 T brown sugar
1 t marjoram
1 T chopped parsley
¼ t salt

Pare carrots and cook until tender. Drain and set aside. Melt butter in skillet and blend in remaining ingredients. Add carrots and simmer gently until well glazed. Serves 6.

The strength of the horse, the mule, the goat and the ram, moreover, the strength of the bull [ginseng] bestows on him . . . This herb will make thee so full of lusty strength that thou shalt, when thou art excited, exhale heat as a thing on fire.

— The Atherva Veda,
ancient Indian medical book

GINSENG ASPIC

1 T gelatin
2 cups tomato juice
½ lb. cooked shrimp

Soften gelatin in ¼ cup cold tomato juice. Heat remaining juice and stir in gelatin mixture. Cook over low heat until gelatin is dissolved. When mixture is cooled, stir in shrimp and pour into large ring mold. Chill to set.

For Topping:

1 small package lime gelatin
2 small envelopes ginseng tea
1 cup boiling water
¾ cup cold water
2 t horseradish
1 pt. small curd cottage cheese

Dissolve gelatin and ginseng in boiling water. Add cold water, horseradish and cottage cheese; mix well. Cool lightly and pour on top of chilled tomato mixture. Chill until set. Unmold and serve. Serves 6.

*He that would live for aye
Must eat sage in May.*

— *Old English proverb*

CASSEROLE VERDE

8 large green tomatoes, cut in thick slices
1 lb. sharp cheddar cheese, grated
1 T fresh sage, chopped
   Salt and pepper to taste

Place 1 layer of tomatoes in casserole. Cover with cheese and sprinkle with sage, salt and pepper. Repeat layers until all ingredients are used up. Bake uncovered in 350° oven for 30 minutes. Serves 6.

Nutmegs and ginger nuts which have passed through the digestive canal are irresistible aphrodisiacs.

– Reinhold Gunther,
Kulturgeschichte der Liebe

GINGERBREAD

3 T butter
½ cup sugar
1 egg, beaten
1½ cups sifted flour
1 t ginger
1 t cinnamon
¼ t nutmeg
1 t soda
¼ t salt
½ cup milk
½ cup molasses

Cream butter and sugar and stir in egg. Mix in dry ingredients, milk and molasses. Beat until batter is smooth. Pour into 8 x 8 inch greased baking pan and bake in 350° oven for 25 to 30 minutes.

> *The best times to make love are four to five hours after lunch and four to five hours after dinner.*
>
> *— Dr. Nicholas Venette,*
> **Le Tableau de la Vie Conjugale,**
> *1696*

Aromatic herbs and aphrodisiac recipes judiciously used in the preparation of meals, renew weakened organisms; they bring back to life exhausted feelings, and permit man to enjoy for a long time "those endowments of strength so dear."

—The Squire of Baudricourt

HERB FRIED CHICKEN

1 chicken, jointed
½ cup flour
2 T Parmesan cheese
½ t poultry seasoning
   Salt and pepper to taste
   Olive oil
   Butter

Clean and dry chicken. Combine flour, cheese and seasonings in bag. Shake chicken pieces in bag until well coated. Heat equal parts of oil and butter and fry until done. Serves 4.

NUTMEG: Has marvellous restorative powers when brewed into tea. Nutmeg is a Chinese love spice.

CANARD POUR DEUX

1 1½ lb. wild duck
½ t salt
   Freshly ground black pepper
1 small onion, cut in chunks
1 small apple, cut in chunks
1 stalk celery
3 juniper berries (optional)
2 slices bacon
½ cup dry white white
   Grated nutmeg

Clean duck and sprinkle cavity with salt and pepper. Stuff with onion, apple, celery and berries. Truss bird. Cover duck with bacon slices and sprinkle lightly with nutmeg. Roast in 450° oven for 40 minutes basting frequently with wine. Serves 2.

CELERY SEED: Has been prescribed as a remedy for impotence.

TARTARE STEAK

¾ cup lightly mashed avocado
½ lb. ground steak
1 t Worcestershire sauce
¼ t celery seed
    Salt and freshly ground pepper to taste
1 small onion, thinly sliced
    Capers
    Toast rounds

Mix avocado, meat, Worcestershire sauce, celery seed, salt and pepper. Spread on toast rounds and garnish with onion slice and capers. Serve as Hors d'Oeuvres.

SAVORY: From the Latin satureja, *"plant of the satyrs."*
Savory is a Roman aphrodisiac.

SAVORY MEAT BALLS

¾ lb. ground beef
¼ lb. ground veal
1 small onion, grated
1 small apple, grated
1 egg
½ cup dry crumbs
1 t horseradish
¼ cup water
1 t savory
1 t salt
¼ t pepper
1 cup consomme

Mix all ingredients except consomme. When thoroughly
mixed, form into small balls and simmer in undiluted
consomme for 30 minutes. Serves 4.

MUSTARD SEED: Repeated emersions of the penis in
mustard seed is said to restore virility.

STEAK BUTTER

1 medium onion, grated
4 T minced parsley
2 t Worcestershire sauce
¼ t dry mustard
½ t paprika
5 T butter, softened
   Salt and pepper to taste

Blend ingredients into a smooth paste. Spread on broiled
steaks and serve immediately. Serves 6.

SWEET BASIL: Associated with Erzulie, Hatian voodoo goddess of love, and used extensively in voodoo love magic. In Italy, sweet basil symbolizes love.

VOODOO CASSEROLE

4 center cut pork chops
2 T oil
1 onion, chopped
¼ cup chopped celery
2 cups tomato sauce
1½ cups water
2 T brown sugar
1 t basil
1 cup rice
   Salt and pepper to taste

In large skillet brown chops in hot oil; remove chops. Add onion and celery and simmer until lightly browned. Stir in remaining ingredients and return chops to top of mixture. Cover skillet and simmer for 30 minutes. Serves 4.

ROSEMARY: An old custom of decking the bridal bed with rosemary to insure conjugal bliss still persists in some parts of Europe. Symbolizes remembrance.

HONEYMOON CHICKEN

¼ cup olive oil
2 T lemon juice
1 sprig fresh rosemary
   Salt and pepper to taste
1 chicken, jointed

Combine oil, lemon juice and seasonings. Place chicken in sauce and marinate several hours. Place chicken on grill over hot coals and brush frequently with marinade. Serves 4.

GARLIC: Contains hormones. The Romans hung garlic over their doors to ward off witches.

LIVERS SAUTÉ SEC

¾ lb. chicken livers
2 T butter
2 T olive oil
1 cup sliced mushrooms
1 clove garlic, chopped
2 T chopped onion
1 oz. sherry
1 small avocado, sliced
   Salt and pepper to taste

Heat butter and oil. Saute livers, mushrooms, garlic and onion (about 5 minutes). Pour sherry over livers and saute until livers are cooked and mushrooms are tender. Remove to platter and garnish with avocado. Serves 2.

FENNEL: Fennel seed is considered an aphrodisiac in Mediterranean countries.

> *The brew: rattlesnake's blood. It was drunk 'neat' — through a tiny opening made in the reptile's tail. As one man held up two creepy creatures just below the head, his two friends lay down comfortably on the floor and each grabbing one snake's tail began sucking away. After five minutes, two others took over . . . A 63-year-old who paid $5 to attend one of these sessions, said, "Its [sic] well worth it. I feel young again. Its [sic] better than any Western aphrodisiac I've tried."*
>
> *— Felix Abisheganaden,*
> San Francisco Chronicle
> *Foreign Service, writing about*
> *Malaysian Chinese in*
> *Kuala Lumpur's Chinatown, 1970*

FENNEL FISH SAUCE

1 cup sour cream
1 T lemon juice
1 t sugar
½ t dry mustard
½ t celery salt
¼ t fennel seeds

Combine all ingredients and mix well. Chill. Excellent with cold fish salads. Yields 1 cup.

CARAWAY: If given to a loved one, caraway will prevent infidelity in love. An Oriental aphrodisiac.

ROYAL CARAWAY PIE

1 unbaked 9 inch pastry shell
4 large onions, chopped
1½ T butter
1 cup cooked diced ham
1 cup milk
1 T prepared mustard
1 egg, beaten
½ cup grated caraway cheese

Saute onions in butter until soft. Remove from heat and add ham. Sprinkle cheese in bottom of pie shell and cover with onion mixture. Beat milk, mustard and egg; pour over top. Bake in 375° oven for 40 minutes or until custard is set. Serves 6.

GINGER: A spice lover's and lovers' spice. Ginger is used for erotic purposes in the Near and Far East.

CHILI SAUCE

20 large tomatoes, peeled and chopped
6 large onions, chopped
6 large green peppers, chopped
3 T salt
6 T brown sugar
2 t ginger
3 t cinnamon
½ t ground cloves
6 cups cider vinegar

Mix all ingredients in large kettle and simmer slowly until vegetables are tender and sauce thickens. Stir frequently. Seal in sterilized jars.

CORIANDER: A common ingredient in Middle Ages love potions. Lauded in the Arabian Nights *as an aphrodisiac.*

ICED TOMATOES

20 cherry tomatoes
6 oz. cream cheese, softened
4 T mayonnaise
¼ t dry mustard
1/8 t coriander
    Salt and white pepper to taste

Wash tomatoes and dry thoroughly. Blend cheese, mayonnaise and seasonings to consistency of creamy icing. Frost tomatoes with cheese mixture and place on wax paper to chill. Place tomatoes on toothpicks and serve as Hors d'Oeuvres.

SEXUAL POWER

Positively and Permanently restored in 2 to 10 days, effects in 24 hours; almost immediate relief. No nauseating drugs, minerals, pills or poisons, but the delicious **MEXICAN CONFECTION,** *composed of fruits, herbs and plants. The most* **POWERFUL** *tonic known. Restores the Vigor, Snap and Health of youth. Sealed book free, giving full particulars.*

— 19th century American advertisement

TUMERIC: Primarily used in the preparation of curries, tumeric is highly prized among the Indians as a love stimulant. Also used as a vaginal douche.

CHOW CHOW

4 cups pearl onions, peeled
4 cups small cucumbers
4 cups cauliflower, flowers
3 green peppers, sliced
1 cup salt
4 qts. water
1 qt. vinegar
4 T dry mustard
1 T turmeric
4 T flour
1 cup sugar

Soak vegetables overnight in salt and water. Drain. Cover vegetables with water and boil for 6 minutes. Drain. Boil vinegar and add paste made with mustard, turmeric, flour, sugar and a little cold vinegar. Stir over low heat until mixture thickens. Add vegetables and cook slowly for 10 minutes. Seal in sterilized jars.

SAFFRON: Used by the ancient Phoenicians as a love spice to flavor the moon-shaped cakes eaten in honor of Ashtoreth, the goddess of fertility. Saffron is also a bridal spice.

SAFFRON RING CAKE

1/3 cup butter
2/3 cup sugar
2 eggs, separated
2/3 cup raisins
½ cup chopped walnuts
1/3 cup chopped citron
1¾ cups flour
1½ t baking powder
    Pinch of saffron
¼ t salt
2/3 cups milk

Cream butter and sugar thoroughly and mix in egg yolks. Add raisins, walnuts and citron. Sift dry ingredients 3 times and add alternately to butter mixture with milk. Fold in stiffly beaten egg whites. Pour into greased and floured ring pan. Bake in 350° oven for 1 hour.

CARDAMON: An amatory aid because of its ancient and modern use as a breath sweetener. Cardamon is an Arabian aphrodisiac.

CARDAMON COOKIES

4 eggs
1 cup sugar
8 T butter, melted
2 T heavy cream
1 t cardamon
5 cups flour, sifted
   Oil
   Powdered sugar
   Nutmeg

Beat eggs and sugar together. Add butter, cream and cardamon. Stir in flour and mix thoroughly. Place dough on floured board and roll to thickness of pastry crust. Cut in diamond shapes and make slit lengthwise in center. Pull one end through slit. Fry in 3 inches of hot oil until lightly browned. Drain and sprinkle with powdered sugar and nutmeg. Yields 5 dozen.

POTPOVRRI ℣ APHRODISIACS

ODORS

VITAMINS

DRVGS

VIRILE VITAMINS & MINERALS

The relationship between diet and sexuality is immensely complex and as yet not fully understood. Certain foods, however, do contain many vitamins, minerals and elements which have a direct effect on the sexual functions and reproductive organs.

Among the most important minerals and elements which contribute to the efficient functioning of the sex glands are iron, copper, phosphorous and iodine. Vitamins also serve the sexual functions as well as being necessary for general good health. These organic compounds are chemically related to hormones and interdependent with them. Vitamins act on the endocrine glands which in turn act on the entire reproductive system.

Vitamin A nourishes the mucous membranes which lubricate the sexual organs. Vitamin B_1 (thiamine), produces and supplies hormones to the pituitary gland, which stimulates the sex glands, and is essential to estrogen-androgen balance. Vitamin D, the "sun vitamin," can be produced in the skin and is known to increase sexual desire. But of all the virile vitamins, vitamin E, the "antisterility vitamin," is probably the most important to sexuality. Essential to the efficient functioning of all the other vitamins, vitamin E is primarily concerned with the reproductive process. Not discovered until 1922, it is also called "tocopherol," a term derived from the Greek words meaning childbirth.

VIRILE VITAMINS' ELEMENTS & MINERALS

VITAMIN A . . . . calf liver, turnip greens, beet greens, mustard greens, spinach, Hubbard squash, carrots, dandelion greens, kale, collards, cantaloupe, sweet potato, pumpkin, broccoli.

VITAMIN B₁ . . . . soybeans, wheat germ, brown rice, calf and beef liver, brewer's yeast, white flour, skim milk, kidney, oatmeal, beef heart, leg of lamb, whole-wheat flour, peanuts, peas.

VITAMIN D . . . . sunshine, fish and liver oils.

VITAMIN E . . . . spinach, wheat germ oil, eggs, soy oil, peanut oil, kale, corn, corn oil, cottonseed oil, meats, wheat germ, carrots, Brussels sprouts, oatmeal, celery, whole-wheat flour, parsley.

IODINE . . . . fish, shellfish, sea vegetables, iodized vegetable salt.

IRON & COPPER .... oysters, liver, broccoli, beef heart, mustard greens, veal, beef, dandelion greens, chard, beet greens, turnip greens, kale, beans, spinach, lamb, pork, lentils, peas.

PHOSPHOROUS .... fish, oysters, liver, cheese, fowl, veal, heart, brains, sweetbreads, kidney, lamb, beef, pork, beans, milk, lean meat, eggs, oatmeal, lentils, cauliflower, peas, pumpkin, potatoes.

THE BOUQUET OF LOVE

The physiology of smell remains, for the most part, a mystery. An odor can be a fleeting whiff which appears briefly, only to vanish like a spectre, or a lingering, pungent aroma, overpowering in its magnitude. From the satisfying aromas of foods, to the subtle fragrances of exotic perfumes, to the heady effluvia of the genitalia, the scent of love permeates man's very existence.

In all animals the most distinct odors are found in the vicinity of the genitalia, especially during the mating season when animals exude a beckoning odor to attract other animals. Even in the plant world the scent emanates from the reproductive area of the flower. Some of our finest perfumes are made with musk, a pungent substance found in the sex glands of the male musk deer.

Human perspiration has been reputed for ages to arouse sexual desire, especially in women. Many peoples, among them the mountain folk of middle America, steeped handkerchiefs in perspiration, later to be used to wipe the brow of the beloved who swooned at the odor. As man becomes more civilized, his sense of smell seems to regress proportionately. According to Freud: "With the advancement of civilization it is precisely the sexual life which must become the victim of repression. For we have long known what an intimate relation exists in the animal organization between the sexual impulse and the function of the olfactory organ." Folklore echoes Freud's observation on the relationship between sex and the "olfactory organ" with the belief that the size of a man's member can be estimated by the length of his nose. And many a newlywed remembers the phenomenon of "brides' cold," sniffles caused by intense sexual excitement.

We all like to smell good. The trouble is that what smells "good" in one society may smell "bad" in another. The pleasantness or unpleasantness of an odor seems to be more of a social than a physical matter. In modern, civilized societies we are led to believe that a man or a woman must smell like anything *but* a human being. The scent of perfumes, colognes and deodorants fill the air. In order to attract a member of the opposite sex, a woman must smell like a rose, a man like old spice. But the fact remains that the most powerful scent of love is the body's own natural odor. The 17th century English poet, Robert Herrick, has penned a pungent tribute to his truelove's essence:

> Would you oil of blossoms get?
> Take it from my Julia's sweat:
> Oil of lilies and of spike,
> From her moisture take the like;
> Let her breathe or let her blow,
> All rich spices thence will flow.

RX FOR LOVE

ABSINTHE

Wormwood *(Artemisia absinthium)*, is so named because it was dedicated to Artemis, the ancient Greek goddess of the hunt and the moon. Absinthe is a green liquor from France containing oils of wormwood, anise, marjoram and other aromatics. Absinthe may make the heart grow fonder, but its repeated use can lead to insanity and even death.

AMANITA MUSCARIA

A poisonous hallucinogenic mushroom common to Mexico and Colombia. Amanita muscaria was used as a sacrament in ancient fertility rites, and was symbolic of the erect penis. Even today, many Indian tribes consider this mushroom to be sacred.

BELLADONNA

The Deadly Nightshade *(Atropa belladonna)*. A narcotic is extracted from the juice of the berry which contracts the pupils of the eyes, making them "sparkle." Although used extensively in witches' brews and love potions, the aphrodisiac properties of the drug are doubtful.

DAMIANA

A drug made from the plant *Turnera diffusa,* found in Mexico, and reputed to cause direct genital stimulation. The Aztecs used the leaves of the damiana plant during their rituals of peace and love. Damiana, a yellowish liqueur, dubbed "The Liqueur for Lovers," is available in the United States.

DAWAMESC

An aphrodisiac made in Algiers, consisting of hemp, sugar, cinnamon, cloves, cardamon, musk, nutmeg, pine kernels, pistachios and orange juice.

HASHISH

An intoxicating preparation made from the resin of the *Cannabis sativa*. Hashish, and the less potent part of the plant, marijuana, can be smoked or eaten. *Charas,* Indian hashish, is made into a sweetmeat called *maajun*. In America, hashish is baked into brownies and other sweetmeats. Hashish, and to a lesser degree, marijuana, tend to intensify sensations and prolong coition. According to Hector France, "Hashish is of course a positive aphrodisiac, the length of the venereal act being at once reinforced and repeated." The possession of hashish and marijuana is illegal in many countries, including the United States.

L-DOPA

A drug used to treat Parkinson's disease, with aphrodisiac side-effects. A university professor in his late 60's who was being treated with L-dopa became an exhibitionist in the hospital and raped his wife when she came to visit him.

NUX VOMICA

Made from a Southeast Asian tree, *Strychnos nux-vomica,* having poisonous seeds used in making brucine and strychnine. Although said to have aphrodisiac properties, nux vomica is a lethal poison.

OPIUM

A narcotic made from the dried juice of the opium poppy which can be smoked or eaten. According to Dr. Albert Ellis, "Opium and its derivatives, contrary to popular belief, acts as a deterrent to sexual desire as it deadens the nervous system."

PCPA

Known technically as p-chlorophenylalanine, PCPA has been used to reduce the body's production of serotonin, a substance suspected of contributing to schizophrenia. PCPA was given to laboratory rats who showed a marked increase in sexual activity. One woman who was being treated with the drug temporarily turned into a raving nymphomaniac, leading scientists to suspect that the drug may be a "true" aphrodisiac.

SPANISH FLY

(Cantharides). A preparation made from ground European blister beetles, *Lytta vesicatoria.* Spanish fly acts as a painful irritant to the sexual organs, and can cause death, even in minute quantities. One American folk tale, often repeated, relates that a young girl, after having Spanish fly slipped into her drink, was sent into such heat that she copulated with the gear shift knob in her boyfriend's automobile.

VIGOSAN

A patent medicine sold in Europe, but unavailable in the United States. Vigosan is composed of 2mgm. testosterone, 5 mgm. yohimbine, 60 mgm. extract of damiana, 5 mgm. nux vomica, 0.37 mgm. strychnine, and 10 I.U. vitamin E.

YOHIMBINE

A yellowish poisonous alkaloid, derived from the bark of the *Corynanthe yohimbe,* or yohimbe tree. Yohimbine has been used for centuries by Africans and South Americans as an aphrodisiac. In South America, yohimbine is called *quebrachine.*

BIBLIOGRAPHY

Adams, Leon D. *Commonsense Book of Drinking.* New York: David McKay Co., Inc., 1960

Anand, Mulk Raj. *Kama Kala. Geneva:* Nagel Publishers 1962

Apicius, *The Roman Cookery Book.* Trans. Barbara Flower, and Elisabeth Rosenbaum. London: George G. Harrap & Co., Ltd., 1958.

Baroja, Julio Caro. *The World of the Witches.* Chicago: U. of Chicago Press, 1965.

Bauer, W.W., M.D. *Potions, Remedies and Old Wives' Tales.* Garden City, N.Y.: Doubleday & Co., Inc., 1969.

Bey, Pilaff (pseudonym). *Venus in the Kitchen.* Ed. Norman Douglas. London: William Heinemann, Ltd., 1952.

Bishop, George. *The Booze Reader.* Los Angeles: Sherbourne Press, Inc., 1965.

Bloch, Dr. Iwan. *Odoratus Sexualis.* New York: American Anthropological Society, 1933.

Brillat-Savarin, Jean Anthelme. *The Physiology of Taste.* Trans. M.F.K. Fisher. New York: The Heritage Press, 1949.

Connell, Charles. *Aphrodisiacs In Your Garden.* New York: Taplinger, 1965.

Culpeper, Nicholas. *Culpeper's Complete Herbal.* New York: Sterling Publishing Co., Inc., 1959.

Davenport, John. *Aphrodisiacs and Anti-aphrodisiacs.* New York: Award Books, 1970.

Davenport, John. *Aphrodisiacs & Love Simulants.* New York: Lyle Stuart, Inc., 1966.

de Givry, Grillot. *Witchcraft, Magic & Alchemy.* Trans. J. Courtenay Locke. London: George G. Harrap & Company, Ltd., 1931.

De Rachewiltz, Boris. *Black Eros.* Trans. Peter Whigham. New York: Lyle Stuart, 1964.

De Ropp, Robert S. *Drugs and the Mind.* New York: Grove Press, 1957.

Douglas, Norman. *Paneros.* Private Edition: No. 14 of 780. Collection of Marshall Blum, Hillsborough, California.

Ellis, Albert, and Abarbanel, Albert (ed.). *The Encyclopedia of Sexual Behavior.* New York: Hawthorn Books, Inc., Publishers, 1961.

Ellis, Albert, Ph. D. *The Art and Science of Love.* New York: Lyle Stuart, 1960.

Ellis, Albert, Ph. D. *The Folklore of Sex.* New York: Charles Boni, 1951.

Ford, Clellan S., and Beach, Frank A. *Patterns of Sexual Behavior.* Harper & Brothers, Publishers, 1951.

Frazer, Sir James (ed.) *The Golden Bough.* New York: Citerion Books, 1959.

Gifford, Edward S., Jr. *The Charms of Love.* Garden City, N.Y.: Doubleday & Company, 1962.

Heartman, Charles F. *Cuisine de l'amour.* New Orleans: Gourmet's Company, 1942.

Henriques, Fernando. *Love In Action.* New York: Dell Publishing Co., Inc., 1962.

Hill, Douglas. *Magic and Superstition*. New York: The Hamlyn Publishing Group, Ltd., 1968.

Jameson, Eric. *The Natural History of Quackery*. Springfield, Ill.: Charles C. Thomas Publisher, 1961.

Klaf, Franklin S., M.D., and Hurwood, Bernhardt J. *A Psychiatrist Looks At Erotica*. New York: Ace Books, Inc., 1964

Leake, Chauncey D., Ph. D., and Silverman, Milton, Ph.D. *Alcoholic Beverages in Clinical Medicine*. Chicago: Year Book Medical Publishers, Inc., 1966.

Legman, G. *Oragenitalism: Oral Techniques in Genital Excitation*. New York: The Julian Press, Inc., 1969.

Legman, G. *The Horn Book*. New York: University Books, Inc., 1964.

Lehmann, Friedrich. *Rezepte der Liebesmittel*. Heidenheim: Erich Hoffmann Verlag, 1955.

Licht, Hans. *Sexual Life in Ancient Greece*. New York: Barnes & Noble, Inc., 1963.

Malla, Kalyana. *The Ananga Ranga*. New York: G.P. Putnam's Sons, 1964.

Maple, Eric. *Magic, Medicine and Quackery*. London: Robert Hale, 1968.

Marcadé, Jean. *Eros Kalos*. Geneva: Nagel Publishers, 1962.

Marcadé, Jean. *Roma Amor*. Geneva: Nagel Publishers, 1961.

Mathison, Richard. *The Shocking History of Drugs*. New York: Ballantine Books, 1958.

Nefzawi, Shaykh. *The Perfumed Garden of the Shaykh Nefzawi.* Trans. Sir Richard F. Burton. New York: G.P. Putnam's Sons, 1964.

Packard, Vance. *The Sexual Wilderness.* New York: David McKay Co., Inc., 1968.

Radford, E., and M.A. *Encyclopedia of Superstitions.* London: Hutchinson of London, 1961.

Rocco, Sha. *Ancient Sex Worship.* New York: Commonwealth Co., 1904.

Tabori, Paul. *A Pictorial History of Love.* London: Drury House, 1966.

The Lucayos Cook Book. Nassau: Old Authors Farm, 1959.

Van de Velde, Th. H., M.D. *Ideal Marriage.* New York: Random House, 1965.

Van Gulik, R.H. *Sexual Life in Ancient China.* Leiden: E.J. Brill, 1961.

Vatsyayana. *Kama Sutra.* New York: Castle Books, 1963.

Wallnofer, Heinrich, and Von Rottauscher, Anna. *Chinese Folk Medicine.* Trans. Marion Palmedo, New York: Crown Publishers, Inc., 1965.

Wedeck, Harry E. *Dictionary of Aphrodisiacs.* New York: The Citadel Press, 1962.

Wedeck, Harry E. *Love Potions Through the Ages.* New York: The Citadel Press, 1963.

Wells, Evelyn. *Champagne Days of San Francisco.* New York: D. Appleton-Century Company, Inc., 1939.

X***, Dr. Jacobus. *The Genital Laws.* Paris: Maison d'Editions Scientifiques, 1900.

INDEX